The World's Best Places

The World's Best Places

Classroom Explorations
in Geography &
Environmental Science

MIKE GRAF

HEINEMANN
Portsmouth, NH

Heinemann
A division of Reed Elsevier Inc.
361 Hanover Street
Portsmouth, NH 03801–3912
www.heinemann.com

Offices and agents throughout the world

Special thanks to Kathleen McFarren for rendering the World's Best Places map in Figures 2–1 and A–1.

Library of Congress Cataloging-in-Publication Data
Graf, Mike.
    The world's best places : classroom explorations in geography & environmental science / Mike Graf.
      p. cm.
    ISBN 0-325-00003-4
    1. Social sciences—Study and teaching (Elementary)—United States. 2. Science—Study and teaching (Elementary)—United States. 3. Project method in teaching. 4. World Heritage areas. I. Title.

LB1584 .G675 2000
372.3'5044—dc21
                                          00-027771

Editor: Leigh Peake
Production: Elizabeth Valway
Cover design: Joni Doherty
Manufacturing: Louise Richardson

Printed in the United States of America on acid-free paper
04 03 02 01 00 VP 1 2 3 4 5

This book is dedicated to all my former students—classroom national park rangers. Your enthusiasm for our study of the World's Best Places has made this project worthwhile. All your pictures, sample projects, and videotapes of past national park fairs that I have collected have allowed me to put this book together. I hope all of you will be able to visit some of these spectacular places.

Also, during my travels around the world I met and stayed with people who helped me see some of each country's incredible scenic preserves. I want to thank each of you for your hospitality and knowledge of your country's national parks. You brought me to the World's Best Places and that makes you, for me, the world's best people.

Contents

· ·

95 Appendix B The National Park Fair

*First section of this appendix introduces the national
park fair.*

107 Appendix C Related Organizations

Gives names and addresses of organizations.

Introduction

. . . .

Welcome to the World's Best Places! The book you are holding in your hand celebrates the most beautiful, diverse, and famous protected lands around the world: the popular and spectacular World Heritage National Parks designated by the United Nations Education Science and Cultural Organization (UNESCO). Through environmental education activities based squarely on accepted science and social studies curricula, this book provides an opportunity for students in the upper-elementary and middle school grades to explore these pristine and remarkable areas and grow in their appreciation and understanding of the world's diverse cultures and environments.

Several years ago, I took a leave of absence from teaching to pursue writing and travel projects that eventually took me around the globe. I remember vividly one of my first stops, a remote national park in the Malaysian jungle. On the way out, I had a brief layover between buses in a small village where a large Chinese school was located. I walked on the campus, backpack and all, and was immediately surrounded by students.

Cries of "An American, an American!" greeted me. The principal, who was also the school's fourth-grade teacher and who spoke a bit of English, met me on the playground. After a tour of the facilities, I visited his classroom. We talked about where I was from, what I was doing, and the fact that I taught children of the very same age in the United States. The students were drawn into the conversation. I believe that this visit was memorable enough to those students that they will never forget where California and the United States are on a world map. The visit also made me recall a familiar study that revealed that 75 percent of United States school students could not find France on a map.

Later in my trip I was hiking in Australia's Blue Mountains National Park, a park located two hours west of Sydney that was being considered for World Heritage status. Deep in the park's mountain canyons, I came across two classes of fifth and sixth graders on a school excursion. After convincing me that I had gone way too far down to climb back up to the rim above and catch a shuttle bus on time, they offered me a ride back to the hostel where I was staying. It was a wonderful opportunity to spend a couple of hours with ten- and eleven-year-olds from across the globe. The Australian students were incredibly curious and had tons of questions. They also displayed a knowledge of the United States that astounded me. In many cases their comprehension of American politics and geography rivaled mine. As the students discussed one American place and event after another, I started wondering if any of my students could demonstrate the same level of knowledge to an Australian they happened to meet. Could any of us? When those students and I said our good-byes, I vowed that as a teacher I would find some way to bring some of the world into my American classroom. But how?

I continued my journey into the heart of Australia. I climbed Ayer's Rock at Uluru-Kata Tjuta National Park, which is a UNESCO Cultural and Natural World Heritage Site. I stood at sunrise on top of that gigantic red monolith with a 360-degree view of Australia's outback sprawled before me and thought about my travels. I recalled the tumbling glaciers of New Zealand, the towering Himalayas in Nepal, the wild tropical jungles of Thailand, and the crocodile-infested wetlands of Australia's Kakadu National Park. Then I counted all of the national parks I had been to in the United States and abroad. I made a mental list of those I still wanted to visit: the Galapagos, the Serengeti Plain, Los Glaciares at the southern tip of Argentina, the gorilla reserves of Zaire. I realized then how I could help students enjoy learning about the world around them: by offering them a glimpse of the world's best national parks.

My eleven-month journey ended in Europe. By this time I had visited dozens of world parks and preserves, many of them UNESCO sites. Like most world travelers I met, I was already planning where to go next, to see what else was out there—and I wasn't even home yet. But I had also begun to work through this project in my mind.

I wanted students to discover these places through their own exploration. Furthermore, I began to realize that if I combined their studies with activities, experiments, and an awareness of stewardship, while adding the responsibility of presentation and park expertise, the students would become responsible "guides" to these places. They could become real rangers!

Once home, I began to research, write, and sort through all my accumulated stacks of notes. I reviewed all the curricula, brochures, and teacher guides I had gathered from each country and all the park notes I had collected. I wrote away for more information, made phone calls to embassies and tourist agencies, and started compiling what I then realized was not just a unit of study for my fifth-grade class that year but also a book.

UNESCO and World Heritage Status

UNESCO currently lists 630 Cultural and/or Natural World Heritage Sites worldwide (128 of them are natural). *The World's Best Places* focuses on thirty-two of the most popular and accessible of the natural parks. It is fairly easy to acquire information about and travel to these preserves. They represent scenic beauty, geologic history, and intriguing wildlife that students will identify with and that teachers can incorporate into science, social studies, and even language arts curricula.

UNESCO sites are cherished by their host countries. In the United States, we also appreciate our national parks, but most people are generally unaware of the World Heritage status. Some of the World Heritage Sites in the United States include the Grand Canyon, Yosemite, Yellowstone, the Great Smokey Mountains, the Everglades, Olympic, Redwood, Mammoth Cave, Carlsbad Caverns, and Waterton Glacier International Peace Park.

To be considered for World Heritage status, a natural park needs to meet a special list of criteria. It should

1. exist as an outstanding natural example of the major states of the earth's evolutionary processes;

2. exist as an outstanding example of progressive and significant geologic processes, biological evolution, and human interaction with the natural environment;

3. contain superlative natural phenomena including formations, features, ecosystems, beauty, and combinations of natural and cultural elements; and

4. contain the most important and significant natural habitats for threatened species of animals with outstanding universal value from a scientific or conservationist perspective.

New parks are constantly being considered for possible inclusion. At certain times, parks are classified as World Heritage in Danger because of human intrusion, development, or pollution that threatens the features of the park. With this classification come suggestions to correct the problems as well as possible funds and organizational help. If these concerns are not alleviated, it is possible that the park in danger may lose its World Heritage status.

Activities in This Book

I wanted my students—and yours—to have as much of a hands-on experience as possible in their study of the World's Best Places. Therefore, this book is filled with projects and activities that I have tested in my classroom, other classrooms, and through workshops. I've constantly reevaluated, added, and changed things. My hope is that the step-by-step descriptions of each project will take you and your students from curiosity to expertise, from questions to knowledge, and from information to grand classroom displays. In the end, I hope that students will come to love these places as much as I do and to feel empathy for their protection. Maybe some students will eventually extend their study into a career when they get older. Perhaps others will be able to visit the places they studied as children. What better way is there to celebrate the best the planet has to offer?

You'll notice that the activities in this book are divided into chapters dealing with particular topics of study: wildlife, plant life, geography, and geology. This is to help you organize the use of this book according to your own curriculum. For instance, you might want to explore the volcanic activity of a particular park in order to support a science unit on geology or examine the effect of human activity on the environment in order to complement a social studies inquiry. It's entirely up to you—this book is as flexible as you want to make it. You'll find descriptions of the thirty-two UNESCO parks in Appendix A, where the prominent features of each park are highlighted; information on holding your own national park fair in Appendix B; and a list of names and addresses of related environmental organizations in Appendix C. Appendix D contains blank copies of the Project List and Evaluation Form, and the Project Rubric.

Each year, my school holds a national park fair, much like a science fair, based on the research that my student park rangers have conducted on their parks. The fair has grown quite elaborate, with ranger stations, colorful displays and demonstrations, and portfolios of student work. Because this is such a large project, the students are also graded on their work; Chapter 2 will walk you through the process of evaluating student work.

In sum, I hope you and your students enjoy the activities in this book as well as the insights you'll gain about some of the world's best places. Put on your hiking shoes, and take the first step.

1

Teaching in Context and Making Connections

We don't teach in a vacuum. Everything that we convey to our students, from abstract concepts to hands-on experiences, comes wrapped in layers of context. For example, when you present facts about a current event, you also describe events leading up to that event; you might also describe political or weather conditions during the event or public attitudes about it. You may discuss the effects the event could have on people, the environment, future events, and so forth. Imagine that your class is working on a social studies unit on the Civil War; you'd discuss the major factors contributing to the war, people's attitudes toward it, the conditions under which soldiers fought and civilians lived, and the effects that the war had on future generations of Americans. Or suppose you and your class are examining a scientific event such as the explosion of a volcano or the discovery of a new fossil. You'd want to examine what factors led to the volcanic activity or how the fossil discovery was made. These issues represent teaching in context.

Making Connections

With a study of the World's Best Places, you and your students can choose ways to make connections to other subjects. Tarry Lindquist, author of *Seeing the Whole Through Social Studies* (1995, Portsmouth, NH: Heinemann), calls this process of making connections "integrating the curriculum" (6–7). Here are some ways to make connections to the World's Best Places.

Make connections between subject areas by looking for natural links. For instance, studying endangered plant and animal species provides a natural link between science and social studies, in which students can research the human activities that may have led to the endangerment and look at the effect that the disappearance of a species may have on humans. Students can also study cultural attitudes toward preservation in general or toward a certain type of animal or plant. In the meantime, they can research the scientific aspects of endangerment, for instance, by examining the effects of a shrinking habitat. There is also a natural link to language arts, as students may read and write everything from letters of protest to short stories about a particular animal. In fact, I have my students give speeches to different classes about the upcoming national parks fair, giving them public-speaking experience.

Make connections between learning skills by looking for ways in which your students can transfer skills from one discipline to another. For instance, writing a letter to a particular national park to request information about the park combines language arts skills with research skills that are important to science and social studies. Students practice formulating and asking the right questions to obtain the information they need, and they also practice composing a piece of writing.

Make connections to an organizing topic by identifying themes that relate to the topic, such as endangered species or the destruction of the rain forest. As students complete activities dealing with the national parks in this book, you can help them make connections to a larger unit of study, such as glaciers or water pollution.

Make connections by focusing school subjects around a major concept. Your school or grade level may decide to focus an entire school-year curriculum on a major concept or two, such as the preservation of the natural environment. Thus language arts, social studies, science, art, and even math classes will devote some time to units of study that work back to issues surrounding the preservation of the natural environment. Language arts classes may write letters to Congress; social studies classes may study indigenous cultures that are disappearing; science classes may study volcanic activity around the world; art classes may paint murals of habitats; and math classes may examine the declining numbers of certain species and create graphs and charts of their findings.

Teaching Preservation of the Natural Environment

Preserving the natural environment is the context on which this book focuses. I believe that it is vital for us as teachers to educate the next generation of "park rangers"—which students will come to think of themselves as they do the activities in this book—when various wildlife and plant life species begin to disappear from the earth, they cannot be retrieved, and their disappearance threatens our planet's ecosystems. It's difficult to convey this idea to young children—and many adults—because they cannot understand how the disappearance of a species of, say, a small plant across town or a tiny bird half a world away affects them. Why should they—or we—care whether the Florida panther survives or whether a coral reef in Australia remains undisturbed? What does it matter whether an aboriginal rain forest culture is preserved or whether the four hundred species of fish found only in Lake Malawi are allowed to thrive? This is where the importance of context comes in. As teachers, we need to be able to help children understand why the preservation of their environment is so vital to them as individuals. They need to understand that all species on this earth are interconnected, and when one plant or animal is threatened or becomes extinct, it could indicate that other species are in danger.

National Park Fair

As mentioned in the introduction, each year my class holds a national park fair, where students, acting as park rangers, build "ranger stations" that contain a wealth of information in a variety of media about the UNESCO parks they have been studying. (See Appendix B for specific recommendations on how to hold a national park fair at your school.) I can't think of any better way to exemplify the features and issues of the World's Best Places than holding a national park fair. While it is not necessary for you to hold a full-scale fair, it does provide a perfect example of teaching in context. Students are required to draw upon skills across all disciplines, integrating them into one organizing principle.

Projects are the backbone of the national park fair. Students enjoy doing them, and the projects help attract plenty of visitors to the fair. The students conduct background research on their parks, sift through necessary and unnecessary data, write letters, paint posters, juggle percentages and statistics, read about different cultures, conduct experiments to learn about glacier activity, study geologic time, write about the habitats of animals and plants, and so forth. They also learn to work together as a community on a project that comes to mean a great deal to them. Thus, they make connections to every area of academic work as well as to their overall school experience—their learning environment. As a teacher, I am gratified not only to see all these connections being made but also to see them being made toward such an important cause.

Whether you use one activity from this book or you launch a

whole program on conservation, look for ways you can make connections. Be a lightning rod between the environment and your students. Illuminate the context for everything your students study, and they will have a better understanding of the planet on which they live.

2

Getting Started

Narrowing the Focus

You will need to decide how you want to focus your study of the parks, depending upon the connections you want to make with other units of study. If you are studying Africa, you could choose one or more of the African parks such as Garamba National Park in Zaire. If you are studying wildlife in general, you'll want to choose one of the parks known for its wildlife such as Royal Chitwan National Park in Nepal. Students are going to become expert rangers through the study of a park or a feature of the park such as lions or waterfalls.

Background Resources

Before my students begin their study of the World's Best Places, I start by gathering background resources—books, magazines, Internet information, encyclopedias, and videos. Such resources provide a context for students' hands-on projects.

I scour the public library and my books at home to gather whatever I can find on national parks, explorers, conservationists, endangered species, and countries of the world.

Some of my favorite books include international or regional travel guides from publishers like Lonely Planet, Moon Publications, and the Sierra Club. These books have sections on each country's best national parks. *National Geographic* also has videos and books on world parks. *Reader's Digest* and other photo-essay or picture books are usually available from local libraries.

I bring to class some other works, such as John Muir's *My First*

Summer in the Sierra, Wilderness Essays, and *Stickeen: John Muir and the Brave Little Dog.* Other favorite books are John Wesley Powell's *Canyons of the Colorado,* Rachel Carson's *Silent Spring,* Ralph Waldo Emerson's *Nature,* Edward Abbey's *Desert Solitaire,* Henry David Thoreau's *On Walden Pond,* and Farley Mowat's *Never Cry Wolf.* The August 1999 issue of *Outside* magazine published an article titled "Going to the Source" that lists guides, mentors, and teachers who are considered pioneers of regional environmental and recreational movements.

For those of you with access to a computer, the Internet contains a veritable jungle of information. See the websites mentioned in Appendices A and C, or type in keywords such as "UNESCO," "World Heritage List," "World Wildlife Fund," "World Conservation Monitoring Centre," "United States National Parks," "World National Parks," "Earth First," or "Sierra Club."

Encyclopedias on the Internet and on CD-ROM are also available. CD-ROM encyclopedias include *Microsoft Encarta Encyclopedia* from Microsoft Corporation; *Britannica CD* from Encyclopedia Britannica; *Compton's Interactive Encyclopedia* from Compton's Home Library; and *Grolier Multimedia Encyclopedia* from Grolier Interactive.

I also show several nature-related videos in class. The "Exploring America Series" shows many of the parks in the United States, including Yosemite, Yellowstone, Olympic, and the Everglades. The "Silent Safari Series" shows all major wildlife from Africa, such as giraffes, lions, and elephants. "Really Wild Animals" focuses on Australian wildlife. National Geographic also has many great videos.

When we begin our study of the World's Best Places, I share these resources with my students and talk about how we will be using them. I read some of my favorite passages from the books to my students, tag important pages with Post-it Notes, and display the books in class. We also start discussing exploration, conservation, and the passion for study of the natural world.

Introducing the World's Best Places

I now introduce my students to UNESCO and the World Heritage Parks. First, I show them a world map of the World Heritage Parks mentioned in this book (see Figure 2–1).

As we look at the map, we talk about the different natural and cultural reserves, and I ask them if they have heard of any of the parks before. I also ask them why they think the parks are included on the World Heritage list and what could happen to the parks if they were damaged in any way.

The World's Best Places

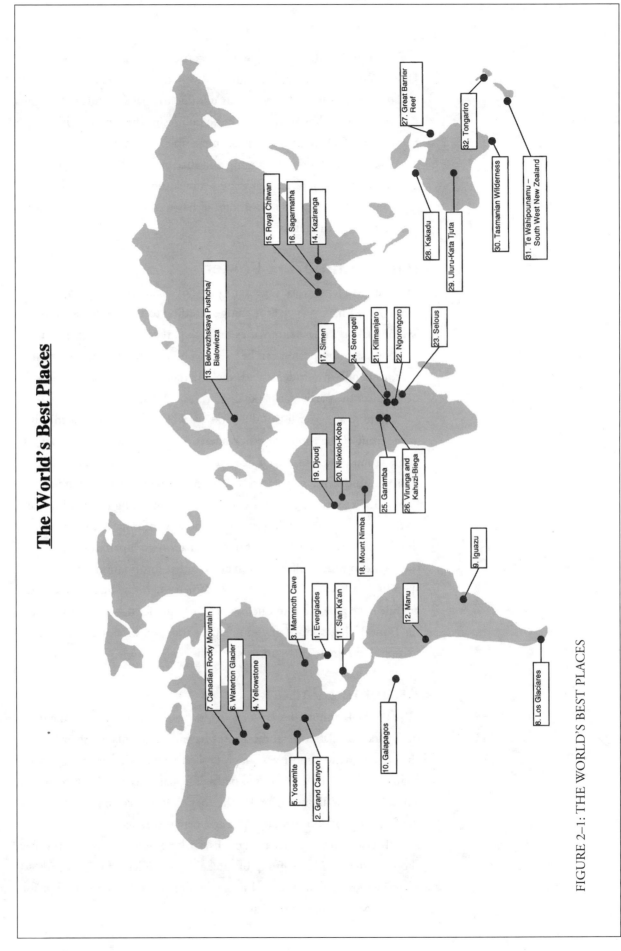

FIGURE 2–1: THE WORLD'S BEST PLACES

13

I point out that in certain areas, particularly the former Soviet Union and parts of Asia, there are relatively few UNESCO parks. I explain that this lack of preserves is not due to a lack of cultural or natural treasures in those areas but to the politics of the region, which made UNESCO status difficult or impossible to attain in the past. I also tell them that this is changing and that because of political changes and the recent explorations of these regions, the doors to these places are opening and there is a possibility of having many more UNESCO designations in the future.

Park Summaries Poster

I have my students work together to quickly create brief summaries of those parks I have selected for study according to the connections we will be making. These summaries for each park, attached together on one big classroom poster, can be used to launch a bit of study on each park, to familiarize students with the different parks, and to help students select the particular parks they wish to study.

I create a master list of the parks we will study, and I post this list at the front of the room for quick reference. I set out sheets of paper on tables around the room, each headed with the name of one park that the class will study. In a sort of free-for-all, the students look through all the books and resources I have provided—including taking turns using the computer to explore the Internet—to find any information they can on the selected parks. When they find information on a particular park, they write in brief, bulleted summaries of that information on the corresponding park sheet (see Figure 2–2). When the individual park sheets are filled, we glue them to one big piece of butcher paper and I post it in the front of the room. If any individual park sheet has little or no information, I eliminate that park from the list.

Assigning Parks

I use the Park Summaries Poster to review with my students all the possible parks the class will study. Then I have the students list their top choices and write a short paragraph explaining why they want to become a ranger for each of their chosen parks. The paragraph can tell me briefly what they know about the park, why they're interested in it, and why they'll do a good job in studying it and being its ranger.

I review the students' paragraphs, making note of which parks they chose. I usually assign a group of three to four students for each park, so I consider group dynamics as I make the final park assignments. The following day, I announce the park assignments.

Kakadu National Park, Australia

- Crocodiles
- Aboriginal rock art
- Poisonous snakes
- Exotic wildlife
- Great birding and wetlands
- Mangrove swamps

- Waterfalls and swimming holes
- Tropical monsoons
- Frill-necked lizards
- Flying foxes

FIGURE 2–2: SAMPLE PARK SUMMARY A Sample of a Park Summary, which can also include a few pictures and a map of the park.

Talking About the Parks

After the students have been assigned their parks, it is a good time to introduce the concepts of park empathy, pride, stewardship, and responsibility. I talk to the students about knowing and appreciating their chosen parks. The parks and their features are dependent upon the students; the world's environment and sustainability may very well be associated with environmental issues and the preservation of special places.

Here is an example of recent events at a UNESCO park that I have talked about with my classes. Every year, I attend the Banff International Film Festival that tours the best outdoor films of the world. One of the most interesting recent films was a documentary on the mountain gorilla reserves in the Virunga and Kahuzi-Biega National Parks in Zaire, Africa. The movie was put together by a journalist who had studied these magnificent gorillas and followed a family group for years. The lifestyle of the gorillas was thoroughly documented. Unfortunately, there are only about two hundred to three hundred of these gorillas left in the wild, and recent events have left the fate of the remaining gorillas in serious jeopardy. Wars in surrounding countries have driven literally thousands of refugees to camp on or near the mountains where the last of these gorillas live. For the first time, gorillas are regularly encountering humans and vice versa. Now the gorillas are being poached for body parts (hands) in black market trade, and as the refugees rapidly strip the rain forest, they are depleting the gorilla's food supply and their natural habitat.

I emphasize to my students that somehow, by learning about a particular park and its issues, they can become park stewards and perhaps their knowledge and future activism will help the gorillas or help resolve whatever other critical issues threaten each park. And yes, each park has its own unique dilemmas that students can learn about and then address by promoting responsibility and activism.

World's Best Places Map

I create a large world map on which my students locate their parks and draw in park symbols. I also have them color in the different biomes on the map. See Appendix A or Figure 2–1 for a map of the parks included in this book.

To make the world map, I first tape a sheet of white butcher paper onto a large, cleared space on a wall in the classroom or a multipurpose room. I use an overhead projector to project a transparent copy of a world map onto the butcher paper, distancing and focusing the projector as needed. I trace an outline of the continents onto the butcher paper. At the top of the map, I write, "The World's Best Places."

After completing the map outline, I have my students add information. Over the next week, the students use stencils to neatly write in the names of the countries in which their parks are located and the names of their parks. They also select the single most important park feature—such as a land feature, an animal, or a plant—that best symbolizes their chosen park. I have them get my approval for whatever symbols they select. Then they make a picture of the chosen park feature, either by drawing it or copying an illustration or photograph of it, and they attach the picture near its corresponding park on the map. The pictures need to be an appropriate size to fit on the map. Here are some

Park	Symbol
Yellowstone	Old Faithful geyser
Royal Chitwan	Bengal tiger
Kakadu	crocodile
Sagarmatha	Mount Everest
Great Barrier Reef	coral reef

parks and sample symbols:

We've also shaded in the biomes of the world on the map so students can recognize the different climates of their parks. This gets students thinking about specific characteristics and features for which they are becoming the virtual caretakers. They lightly shade the biomes in on the map using colored pencils. Each biome is represented by a standard color, and these colors can be researched by looking at atlases or the Koppen Climate Classification. I have my students create a color key for the biomes and post it to the side of the map.

Research Topics

Now I introduce specific research topics on which my park rangers can focus. I list these topics under the heading "What Rangers Need to Know" because the information is what real rangers have expertise in. You and your own students will need to select topics based on some of the connections you want to make to a larger unit of study or to other disciplines.

Here are some topics that my students and I have come up with:

Topics	Subtopics
geology	caves, mountains, canyons, formations, geothermal heating and energy, geological periods, natural history, changes
park legends and history	stories, cultures, meaning, scientific versions of geologic history
indigenous cultures	use of park, problems, legends, rock art, sacred grounds, hunting and grazing rights
endangered species	habitats, ecosystems, threats, endemics, related products, reintroductions, solutions, organizations
plants	edible plants, poisonous plants, habitats, zones, related climates
animals	examples of highlight, rare, threatened, endangered, or extinct species; characteristics
migration	routes, problems
habitat destruction	causes, solutions, what we can do
visitor information	traveling, prices, vaccinations, accommodations, foods, packing needs, regional concerns, dangers, weather, visas, park catalogs and information, safety information including preventions and treatments
scenery	popular attractions, causes, locations
organizations	issues, journals, ways to connect

Park Letters

In order to gather some of the information on the research topics, as soon as possible, I have my students write letters to the parks, their host countries, regional tourism information centers, and various related environmental organizations (see Appendix C). Each organization will provide overlapping and complementary information, so a student can send a copy of the same letter to different places. My students enjoy doing this letter writing, and they of course eagerly await responses.

It is important that these letters get sent out early in the study of the World's Best Places because the information they receive will help kick off all student research. It may take as much as a month or two to get responses to letters sent overseas; therefore, if you can use e-mail instead, you'll have a quicker turnaround.

We go through a normal letter-writing process, including setting up the return address, date, greeting, body, and closing. The body of the letter consists of an introduction, an explanation of the project, and a request for information on the different research topics. I also have the students edit their letters and encourage final letters to be typed. I review each letter before it is mailed. We want prompt, professional, thorough responses, so I encourage and expect the best possible letters from each student.

When packets and information arrive, you'll be delighted by your students' enthusiasm. In most cases students will receive sufficient responses to these requests, and often responses will list further resources. Once your students have all of their information, it is time for them to specifically review the information and start developing their activities and projects.

Background Research

Reinforce with your students the idea that they will need to do background research in their study of the parks. In order to conduct background research, your students will need to know how to summarize or gather what is most important from their various resources, shorten it, and write it into their own words. Otherwise, students will find gobs of information on a topic and just copy it directly onto notepads or cards.

To demonstrate how to summarize information, I usually make an overhead copy or two of a sample section from the various park pamphlets that have come in. As a class, we read the information together and highlight key words and phrases. Because I have my students summarize their information on 5 x 7" index cards, we next practice summarizing the highlighted pamphlet information onto research cards.

I also have the students write a few sample summaries of their

Kakadu's Animals			
Animal	Physical Description	Food	Habitat
saltwater crocodile (estuarine crocodile)	• long snout • up to 7 meters long • scales on back and neck • gray-brown color with yellow sides • lives up to 100 years	fish, turtles, birds, and other animals	coastal and river areas
loggerhead turtle	• large head • can weigh up to 300 pounds • dark reddish-brown head and upper shell • yellow underside	whelks (snails), crabs, fishes, sponges, and algae	sand dunes and beaches
frill-necked lizard	• about one meter long • scaly frill neck opens like an umbrella to scare off enemies	insects, spider, and small lizards	tree trunks and branches in tropical to warm temperate forests, woodlands and savanna woodlands

FIGURE 2–3: SAMPLE RESEARCH CARD A sample of a research card on a given topic.

own, and I monitor their work to be sure they understand the process. Once I'm convinced students are able to summarize information in their own words, I have them spread out all their sources of information and search for the different research topics we had decided upon (see "Research Topics" on pages 17). I give the students yellow sticky notes that they can use to tag the various topics in their park information packets so they can easily find the information later.

I'll keep monitoring students' progress as they conduct their research. Of course, students will work at different speeds. Some will fill two to three research cards, front and back (see Figure 2–3). Others may struggle. It's important to be flexible and help students find information when necessary. You might also need to review with your students how to summarize. Once some students start accumulating significant amounts of park information in at least a couple of topics, it is time to introduce the projects and activities.

Projects

Depending upon your own purposes and the connections you want to make to other units of study, you can select the type and number of projects and activities you want your class to do. In the following chapters are descriptions of a wide variety of projects, including projects on wildlife, plant life, and geography and geology. If you have decided to hold a national park fair at the end of your study of the World's Best Places, there are many fair projects described in Appendix B.

Once student groups have been assigned their parks, I introduce a few of the projects they will be doing for their study of the World's Best Places. I only introduce a few projects at a time; otherwise my students tend to feel overwhelmed. I also tell my students that projects need to be neat and attractive, just as displays in actual parks are.

Evaluating Students' Projects

When students have started working on projects and activities for the World's Best Places, I introduce the Project List and Evaluation Form (see Figure 2–4). Each student gets a copy of this form, so it makes it easy for me to instantly track the progress of my students. Under the "Projects and Activities" column on this form, the students write in the projects *as we go*. When a rough draft is completed for a particular project, I check off the "Draft Completed" box, and when a final draft is completed I check off the "Final Completed" box. In the "Grade" column, I write in the project's final letter grade, which I take from the Project Rubric (described in Figure 2–5). I use the "Notes" column to write in information for the student, such as compliments about the project or notes telling him or her to redo a project. I always keep a copy of each student's form for myself.

Some projects, activities, and class demonstrations—such as the International Potluck, the whole-class Shrinking Islands activity, and the teacher-demonstrated Lava Flow activity—are ungraded projects that only require a student's participation. For these types of projects and activities, I simply write "completed" under the "Notes" column to show that the student participated.

I use a Project Rubric to evaluate my students' individual projects and activities. When a student has completed a project, I fill out a rubric form while I evaluate the project. I then transfer the grade directly from this rubric to the Project List and Evaluation Form.

During the national park fair, I've had visitors use the Project Rubric form to evaluate rangers' projects. I then collect all the visitors' rubrics for a particular student's project and average all the scores to come up with a final grade for the project.

THE WORLD'S BEST PLACES
Project List and Evaluation Form

Ranger: Sarah Jones   **Park:** Waterton Glacier National Park

Projects and Activities	Draft Completed	Final Completed	Grade	Notes
Introduction Projects				
World Maps	X	X	B	I like your symbol
Park Letters	X	X	0	Please redo
Wildlife Projects				
Endangered Species Posters	X	X	A	
Zoo Dioramas	X	X	A-	Very neat!
Habitat Display Murals	X	X	C	
Migration Stories	X			
Species Game Boards	X			
Thumbprint Biodiversity				
Shrinking Islands	—	—	—	Completed
Plant Life Projects				
Background Research on Plants	X	X		
Plant Identification Posters	X			
International Potluck	—	—	—	Completed
Ecosystem Murals				

FIGURE 2–4: SAMPLE PROJECT LIST AND EVALUATION FORM (A blank form is included in Appendix D).

Geography and Geology Projects				
Visitor Information Pamphlets	X	X	0	Please redo
Travel Essentials Suitcase	X	X	A	
Advance/Retreat Graphs	X			
Geologic Time Line	X			
Freezing Rocks	—	—	—	Completed
Cave Formations				
Wind Erosion				
Park Creation Legends	X			
National Park Fair Projects				
Mission Statements				
Ranger Stations				
Costumes and Uniforms				
Sensory Nature Trails				
Language Posters				
After-the-Fair Projects				
Speeches				
Letter Writing				
Vacation Diaries				
Vacation Game Boards				
FINAL GRADE *(0 = Redo/No Credit)*				

FIGURE 2–4 *continued*

PROJECT RUBRIC

Student: Hannah Millard   **Project:** Zoo Dioramas

Date: **Evaluator:**

DESCRIPTION	SCORE 6 is highest and 1 is lowest; 0 is no credit
Attractive	6
Neat	6
Colorful	4
Realistic illustrations	5
Accurate spelling	6
Relevant information	6
Other	
Total Score	33
Average Score	5.50
Grade*	B

*GRADE: 6 = A 5 = B 4 = B 3 = C 2 = D 1 = F 0 = Redo/No Credit

COMMENTS

Hannah: The class agrees that this is a great diorama!

FIGURE 2–5: SAMPLE PROJECT RUBRIC (A Blank Rubric Form is included in Appendix D.)

3

Wildlife Projects

Students love to study wildlife, especially endangered, threatened, and highlight species and wildlife projects offer many options. Here, more than in any other topic, I present a variety of activities for the students to choose from. First, though, my students and I brainstorm as many topics associated with wildlife as we can think of. We come up with a list that looks like this:

- description of animal
- habitat
- foods
- current population
- threats/status
- lifestyle
- movement/migrations

Then, we'll search all park information for anything related to the park's wildlife. Specifically, we're looking for a list of five to ten of the park's species that are the

- most colorful;
- most interesting;
- most severely threatened; and
- easiest to research.

This list represents the wildlife the students will thoroughly research. They'll focus extensively on two to three of the best of the above animals for their projects. I also expect students to keep a running

Definitions of Wildlife Categories

Highlight—Animals that the park is known for, such as the crocodiles of Kakadu National Park and the grizzly bears at Yellowstone National Park.

Rare—Animals that are hardly ever seen because the population is small.

Threatened—Animals whose population is dwindling because of human intrusion; if trend continues, species could become endangered.

Endangered—Animals whose population is severely reduced; animals have federal protection status and reintroduction programs usually exist.

Extinct—Animals that no longer exist in the wild, in their particular area, and/or anywhere on Earth.

Reintroduced—Extinct or nearly extinct animals that are being returned by humans in order to help promote a healthy breeding population and ecosystem.

FIGURE 3–1: WILDLIFE CATEGORY DEFINITIONS

list of other wildlife in their park.

Next, we'll discuss the need for preservation of habitat and the issues that threaten the survival of wildlife. I ask my students to find out what animal is most threatened at their park and why. They will need this information for their Endangered Species Posters.

Figure 3–1 outlines the definitions of wildlife categories. The list of threatened wildlife worldwide is long. A current list of crucial conservation issues and threats to wildlife can be obtained from the National Parks Conservation Association, the World Wildlife Fund, UNESCO's World Heritage List in Danger, or a number of other wildlife-related organizations.

Endangered Species Posters

I like the Endangered Species Poster to be the first project my class works on. I have used the one-horned Indian rhinoceros in Nepal's Royal Chitwan National Park as an example for this project. Only about

INDIAN RHINOCEROS
of
Royal Chitwan National Park

Endangered   Eats grasses and twigs

Poached for horn   Only about 400 remain

Lives in forest near swamps and rivers

FIGURE 3–2: SAMPLE ENDANGERED SPECIES POSTER

four hundred of these noble creatures remain in relatively few wild sanctuaries. Poaching and habitat destruction as well as a depleted gene pool are the animal's biggest current threats.

Students look through their park information packets to find pictures of the animals they will use for their posters. Once they decide on an animal, they can turn to nature books for more information. Students either trace the animal or copy and enlarge a picture of it. The picture is then placed onto a sheet of 11 x 17" construction paper. We include the following information on the poster:

- name of the animal
- name of the preserve it is in
- its current status (threatened, endangered, etc.)
- threats to the animal
- its habitat
- its current worldwide population
- its migratory pattern

Information can be listed around the picture, on lines at the bottom, or in a box or key. I leave this up to the students. I always have the students do a rough-draft sample of the information before I give them their final poster paper. This avoids wasting the good paper on preliminary drafts.

Zoo Displays and Dioramas

Zoos are considered controversial. Many people feel that zoos are humiliating places in which to display and house many of the world's most exotic and threatened species. It's hard to disagree. However, therein lies the need of zoos. They are places where people can obtain knowledge about these species, knowledge that is crucial to the species' survival. Also, zoos often provide shelter for animals that are unable to care for themselves in the wild because they were hurt or abandoned. Finally, and this is most important for students to know, many zoos are involved in breeding endangered species and releasing them back into the wild.

With this in mind, an excellent activity to support the wildlife study of national parks is a trip to a nearby zoo. If your school isn't within a reasonable distance of a zoo, you can write letters to a zoo and adopt an animal. When you adopt an animal, you typically send money—from $20 to $100 a year or more, depending upon the animal—to the zoo, and in return, it sends your class a picture of the animal. Also, to show that your class has adopted a specific animal, the zoo will usually display the name of your class on a plaque. When my classes have adopted animals, we earned the money for it by having several class fund-raisers during the year.

Once my students have visited a zoo, or received letters and information back from one, I have them make dioramas showing how a zoo is housing a threatened or endangered animal. Dioramas are made in shoe boxes or slightly larger boxes (18 x 24"). Background habitat features can be created to fit the environment that the animal naturally lives in. The foreground can include the animal itself, its prey, and its type of home (den, tree, etc.).

Information about the animal can be posted on a professional-looking zoo-type sign at the side of the diorama. This information can include the following:

- habitat setup
- reproduction
- what country, countries, regions, or UNESCO reserves the animal is now found in
- status in the wild
- plans for reintroducing the animals into the wild

Wildlife Stories

I have each of my students research a favorite animal in his or her park, and make observations and notes about an imaginary encounter with that animal. I got the idea for this project one time when I was able to safely observe a grizzly bear and her cub in Waterton Glacier International Peace Park.

I have each student research to find out the following information about his or her animal:

- its habitat
- what it eats
- where you would see it in the park
- typical antics and daily activities (For example, koalas spend most of their day asleep in a eucalyptus tree because the tree's leaves are the only thing they eat and the chemicals in the leaves sedate them.)

I then have my students gather up journals and pencils, and I take them to a quiet area outside—either the school playground, someone's backyard, or a park—for an imaginary animal observation. I start with some little warm-up exercises, during which I have the students take turns describing what they see, feel, hear, and smell, and if there are birds or other animals nearby, I ask them to describe them in detail, including what the animals look like, what they are doing, what sounds they are making, and so on. Then I ask my students to close their eyes and imagine that they are rangers or naturalists in their own parks and that they are hiking along one of the trails. Suddenly, they see their chosen animal—at a safe distance away. I ask them to imagine the details of the animal they are pretending to observe in the wild: what the animal looks like, what it does, how it sounds, how it smells, what other animals are around. After a few minutes, I ask my students to open their eyes and write notes about their imagined animal observations in their journals. I encourage them to write as much as they can, use plenty of detail, and be as realistic as possible. They can even include a dangerous element, such as an encounter with a crocodile, but I also have them write what they need to do to be safe.

After they have written their notes, I have my students go through the normal writing, editing, and revising process. After they complete their final drafts, I have them share their stories with the class.

Habitat Display Murals

Imagine the walls of your classroom or multipurpose room filled with evergreen forests, lush jungles, sandy deserts, snowy mountains, and azure seas of colorful coral. By creating Habitat Display Murals, your students can bring these habitats as well as others alive for your school. You can do these murals in two ways. One is to designate each wall of the classroom as a different habitat—rain forest, mountain, desert, ocean, and so on. Or, you can divide students into theme groups and have those groups work together to decorate the cafeteria's multipurpose walls according to their habitat. This is when parent volunteers can be a big help! The following are ideas for creating some different types of habitats.

Create a forest by first attaching a large sheet of green butcher paper to the wall. The students can work individually or in small groups to add features of the forest, including the following.

- **Trees:** One way to make a tree is to cut out a tree shape from two layers of paper, paint the outer-facing side of each sheet with green paint for the leaves and brown paint for the trunk and branches, then staple the edges of the papers together, leaving an opening to stuff the tree with crumpled newspaper. Another way to make a tree is to tear off a long sheet of brown butcher paper, twist it around and around to form a thick, course tree trunk, attach it to the floor, wall, and ceiling, and add leaves made of green butcher paper or tissue paper.

- **Vines:** String green tissue-paper leaves on brown yarn and attach the yarn up the wall and across part of the ceiling.

- **Large Animals:** Crumple newspaper into specific animal shapes and tape to hold. Papier-mâché over this shape: dip torn strips of newspaper into a mixture of one part white flour and one part water, then cover the shape with the moistened strips. When the papier-mâché is thoroughly dry, paint it with tempera paint. Add features to the animal using scraps of paper, fabric, pipe cleaners, buttons, and so on.

- **Small Animals and Larger Birds:** Cut out an animal shape from two layers of paper, paint the front of the top layer and the back of the bottom layer, then staple and stuff the animal. Hang the animals in front of the background.

- **Nest of Birds:** For the nest, glue toothpicks onto a circle of brown paper. For each baby bird, cover a cotton ball with colored tissue paper and glue on sequin eyes.

- **Insects:** Cover Styrofoam packing pieces with colored tissue paper, then attach pipe cleaners for legs and toothpicks for the antennae.

- **Butterflies:** Cut butterfly bodies from poster board, and make wings out of colored tissue paper.

- **Web of Spiders**: Make a web by attaching strings to the wall and ceiling. Spiders can be made out of large black or brown pom-poms with pipe cleaners attached for legs.

Create a jungle by first attaching a large sheet of white butcher paper to the wall. On the paper, have the students sketch in a jungle scene—including trees, vines, and animals—then outline the items with crayon or markers and paint them in with watercolors. Plants and animals, created similarly to those previously described for the forest habitat, can also be added.

Create a seascape by first covering the wall with white butcher paper. Students can paint the paper with a wash of watered-down blue and green tempera paint. Sea plants can be made from twisted tissue paper, and they can be attached to the painted paper. In front of the seascape backdrop, hang fish from strings attached to the ceiling. Fish can be made by first papier-mâchéing over balloons of various sizes and shapes, then painting and decorating the papier-mâchéd shapes. Other sea animals can be made by cutting out shapes from fabric scraps of various colors and textures, filling the shapes with stuffing, and hand sewing them together.

Footprint Match Poster

Have your students create Footprint Match Posters that others would use to try to match footprints to their corresponding animals. First, have your students choose several animals that live in their parks. Then have them draw or trace pictures of the animals down the left side or across the top of a piece of poster board or 11 x 17" construction paper and neatly write the names of the animals underneath the pictures. Down the right side of the poster or across the bottom, draw the footprints of the animals in random order and label them. The footprints should be drawn extra large for the poster, so a note should be included next to each footprint stating its actual size. Field guides are excellent resources for footprint shapes and sizes, as well as other information on the animals. Cover the labels of the footprints with small pieces of paper taped at the top to function as flaps. Display the posters in the classroom and have people guess which footprints belong to which animals. After they guess, they can lift the flaps covering the footprint labels to see if they've guessed correctly.

Migration Route Posters

For this activity, your students map the migration routes of some of the animals in their parks as well as some local animals. Explain to your students that migration occurs when wildlife moves to another area. Animals migrate for food, because of climate changes, and for spawning reasons. Many kinds of wildlife migrate: birds, fish, eels, mammals, reptiles, and even butterflies and moths. Some animals, such as salmon, go through extraordinary feats in order to migrate. Unfortunately, logging, mining, development, and pollution are disrupting many migration routes. As many as one thousand natural bird species are currently threatened with extinction, with much of the threat due to a loss of wetlands or marshes along migration routes. Many UNESCO reserves, including Djoudj National Bird Sanctuary in Senegal, seek to give permanent protection to migrating wildlife. Perhaps the greatest animal migration occurs on the Serengeti Plain of Africa, where such parks as Serengeti National Park, Kilimanjaro National Park, and Ngorongoro Conservation Area—all UNESCO reserves—seek to preserve a fantastic display of migration involving literally millions of animals.

Have your students research the migration routes of some of the animals in their parks, as well as a few in or near your town. On a map, have them draw and label the routes. The students can add information about why the different animals migrate to specific places. They can also explain how these routes are or might be disrupted by humans and what the consequences of this disruption could be. Some disruptions might be road building, dams, development, pollution, and climate changes. The Migration Route Posters can be posted in your classroom.

Migration Stories

For this activity, your students write about the migration of an animal in their park, then they share the migration story with the class and others. First, have your students learn everything they can about the migration route of one particular animal in their park. They should find out about the route it travels, stops it makes along the way, reasons it migrates, the season of travel, the speed of travel, and the distance covered. The students can then write stories about the migration of their animals, either covering a single day of the migration or the entire journey. When your students complete their stories, they can read them to the class. They can also tell their migration stories to younger students at the school; to help make their stories more interesting, they can accompany their stories with flannel board illustrations. I've also had my students read these stories out loud at the park fair.

Endangered, Extinct, and Reintroduced Species Posters

These posters show graphs for each park that compare the numbers of animals that have become endangered, those that have become extinct,

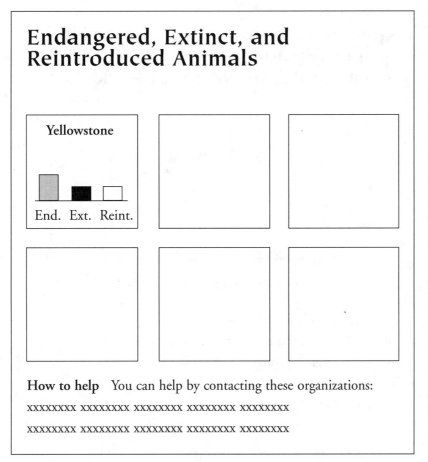

FIGURE 3–3: SAMPLE ENDANGERED, EXTINCT, AND
REINTRODUCED SPECIES POSTER

and those that have been reintroduced over the past ten years. Your students can read through their park information and write to the World Wildlife Fund or other organizations to find out this information. For each park, your students can create a graph with three vertical bars that illustrate the number of animals that have become endangered, those that have become extinct, and those that have been reintroduced into the park. The graphs for all the parks can be combined into one large poster (see Figure 3–3). Students can add a list of organizations that can be contacted to help save the animals.

Species Population Graph Posters

For this activity, your students can graph the population numbers of one particular animal in their park over a long period of time. Have your students find out which animals are struggling to survive in their parks, then have them select one of those animals. They can then find out their animal's population numbers over as many years as possible. Have them graph the population numbers for each ten-year period on a line graph.

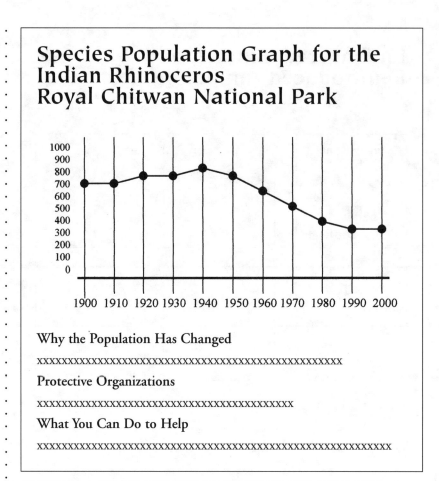

FIGURE 3–4: SAMPLE SPECIES POPULATION GRAPH POSTER

The graphs can be drawn on or attached to posters, and your students can add information about why the population has fluctuated, what organizations are protecting the animal, and what can be done to help the animal (see Figure 3–4).

Endangered Species Concentration

Your students can create a class card-matching game of "Concentration" by making cards related to endangered species. Have your students find out which animals in their parks are rare, threatened, or endangered. With your students, compile a master list of at least twenty of these animals. Then, have your students create three 3 x 5" information cards for each animal. One card shows a picture of the animal in its habitat and gives the animal's name and a brief description of its habitat. Another card shows a picture of the animal's habitat and briefly describes that habitat. The third card names the park where the animal is found and gives a brief description of the general park habitat. Including a reference to the habitat on each card in a set will help the students match the cards during the game (see Figure 3–5).

ANIMAL **Bengal Tiger** lives in jungle and grassland	HABITAT **Grassland** with trees and water courses	PARK **Royal Chitwan** grasslands with rivers flowing out of the Himalayas

FIGURE 3–5: SAMPLE MATCHING ANIMAL, HABITAT, AND PARK CARDS FOR THE "CONCENTRATION" GAME

Combine the sets of cards from all the students into one game of "Concentration." I keep a master list describing each set of cards in case players have trouble matching sets.

To play the game, mix up all the cards and lay them out face down. Players take turns turning over three cards at a time, trying to make a match of all three—the animal, its habitat, and its park. Whenever a player matches all three, he or she can keep the set of matched cards during the rest of the game. When no cards are left to match, the player with the most matching sets wins. Besides having fun playing the game, players will also learn information about the animals.

Endangered Species Game Boards

For this activity, students create board games that are based on one of their park's animals that is threatened or endangered. Have each student select one of the animals in his or her park that is threatened or endangered and learn about the animal's lifestyle, its habitat, its migration route, why it is threatened, and what people can do to help the animal. Once information has been researched, the student can use it to create his or her own game.

The game boards should include a lightly drawn background picture or pictures, which should relate to their park or animal. On top of the background picture, they create a course of about twenty-five one-inch squares that snake across the game board. Students should use rulers to keep lines straight.

When my students create their game boards, I have them start by sketching a rough draft of the game board background and course on an 8½ x 11" sheet of paper. Once I approve the rough draft, I have my students create their game boards on poster board that is approximately 2 x 3'. My students first use pencil to sketch in the background picture and course on the poster board. They also use pencil to write in information in each square, as explained later.

On ten different squares chosen at random along the course, have your students create "move forward" and "take another turn" steps that a player would follow when landing on the selected squares. These squares should contain *positive* information about the animal or park. Some examples could be:

- Get a drink of water—move forward two spaces
- Find a half-eaten carcass—move forward three spaces
- Build a den—take another turn

On five other squares, the students can create "move backward" or "lose a turn" squares that contain *negative* information about their animal or park. Some examples could be:

- A troop of lions preys on the herd—move back two spaces
- The watering hole is dry—lose a turn
- Poachers are in the area—move back three spaces

On all the remaining squares, the students can write in neutral information about the animal or park, such as "The animal's stripes help it hide in the grasslands" or "There is an average of 20 inches of rain a year in the park." When players land on any of these spaces, they simply read the information.

In the squares that make up the course, students can also draw in small pictures that relate to the information they wrote in the square.

After my students create their entire game boards using pencil, I have them play a practice round of the game to see if they are able to finish it in a reasonable amount of time and to see if the information written in the squares is easy to understand. They finalize their game boards by tracing over their pencil lines, drawings, and words with black marking pens. They also color in the background drawing with colored marking pens. We always laminate the finished game boards.

I have my students make the game pieces and draw pictures on them that relate to the animal or the park. For example, game pieces for a Yellowstone Park game may have a grizzly bear, wolf, moose, or bison on it, one for each player. The students can either use store-bought dice or they can make their own dice by cutting patterns from poster board that can be folded into cubes.

To play the game, players roll a die and move their game pieces across the board the correct number of squares. When they land on a square, they read the information in the square and follow any directions. Students can take turns playing one another's games.

What Animal Am I?

In this game, each student tries to guess the name of the animal that is taped onto his or her back. Have each student select the most interesting animal in their park. On a 4 x 6" card, the student writes the name of the animal, draws a picture of it, then lists three to five simple facts about the animal. I then collect all the cards, shuffle them, and tape one card on each student's back with the information side facing out. The students stand in a group and circulate amongst one another, asking questions of other students about their animals to help get clues as to what animal is posted on their backs. The questions can only have "yes" or "no" answers, and the students respond to them based on the information on the cards. Once all the students have guessed which animals they have, they can give brief speeches to the class on the animals.

Animal Smuggling and Poaching Pamphlets

Your students can create pamphlets or posters about animals in or near their parks that have been smuggled or poached. Animals and animal parts are taken from the wild both legally and illegally for trade and profit. Elephant tusks are taken for their ivory, rhinoceros horns are used to make dagger handles, wild cats are killed for their pelts, and live monkeys are taken for medical research. Many of the World's Best Places seek to protect animals from being taken and killed for monetary reasons.

Have your students find out if animals from inside or near their parks have been illegally taken for any reason. Students can also learn why this has been happening and what products are being made from the animals that are taken. Your students can then make a pamphlet or poster showing the plight of these animals. The poster can include information on what can be done to protect the animals. It can also list products to avoid that are made from the animal, and it can list environmental groups and organizations that are trying to help the animal recover.

Whole-Class Activities

Once students are working independently, I like to introduce the following whole-class activities that illustrate important park concepts.

Thumbprint Biodiversity

For this activity, your class creates a poster that shows the different thumbprints of the students.

No two members of any species are exactly alike, just like no two humans are exactly the same. This variation is essential for survival, and it is an important part of the ecosystem. Help your students realize this biodiversity by comparing their thumbprints. Invite each student to make thumbprints of both of his or her thumbs using an inkpad and a sheet of paper. Have students write their names below their set of prints. Display the class set of fingerprints on poster board. Encourage your students to use a hand lens to study the similarities and differences of the thumbprints. You can extend the biodiversity activity by making charts showing comparisons of your students' shoe sizes, eye colors, hair colors, heights, foot widths, finger lengths, and so on.

Shrinking Islands

This activity will help students realize that national parks are islands or sanctuaries for all types of wildlife. Unfortunately, development that encroaches on park borders threatens migration and wildlife, and it leads to overcrowding in the parks. To demonstrate this encroachment, place a long rope or piece of string in a circle on the floor and invite your students to sit comfortably inside it. Make the circle large enough so that there is plenty of extra space around the seated students. Explain to the students that the circle of rope represents a region and that they themselves represent the plants and animals living in that region. Place a smaller circle of rope inside the larger one to represent a national park or wilderness area. Tape the ropes down. Read statements such as those in the following list that describe events that would affect the wildlife corridors represented by the rope outlines, and after each statement, make the outer rope progressively smaller.

- Large developments, such as homes, condominiums, office buildings, and hotels, are being constructed at the park's border.
- Mining is occurring at the at the park's border, making the habitat less suitable for wildlife.
- Pesticide use is causing acid rain, which is polluting water and forests in the park.
- Migrating birds fail to return to the park because their winter habitat has been destroyed.
- Wolves and buffalo are hunted outside the park.
- Cattle grazing outside the park is reducing natural forage.
- Too many boats are chasing away marine life.

Include other statements that are specific to the national parks the students are studying. Whenever the rope touches a student, he or she becomes "extinct" and leaves the circle. After many species have become "extinct," discuss the results with your students. Brainstorm ways to prevent the destruction of these natural areas.

Shrinking Habitats

This activity will help your students understand a park's role in preserving biodiversity. Students will also see how biologically diverse wildlife habitats are shrinking. Place a long rope on the ground or floor in the shape of a large circle. Invite your students to stand just outside this circle. Encourage your students to choose any wild plant or animal they would like to be and to wear a name tag that states the name of their plant or animal.

Place five Frisbees upside down inside the circle. The Frisbees represent national parks where habitats have remained wild. Distribute twenty Popsicle sticks (for a class of thirty) amongst the five Frisbees. The popsicle sticks represent food or habitat that allow the plants and animals to thrive. Invite the students to walk or jog around the outside of the rope circle. When you shout, "Go home!" the students must move quickly inside the circle and try to grab a Popsicle stick. Remind your students not to push or shove each other. Those who do not get a stick have become "extinct," so they are out of the game. Reduce the number of Popsicle sticks by five, then repeat the game. Continue reducing the Popsicle sticks by five and repeating the game until no sticks are left.

Explain to your students that the first round of the game represented a habitat that is in a nearly complete wilderness state. The next two rounds represent habitats that have been reduced because of agriculture, development, and deforestation. The Frisbees represent national parks where habitats have remained wild.

4

. . . .

Plant Life Projects

The plant life of world national parks offers many opportunities for student research projects. When we think of endangered species we often think of wildlife, but plants and forests are also threatened, and many of the world's plants and trees are dying. In many cases, World Heritage Parks house some of the last habitats for threatened or rare plants.

After talking to my class about the importance of plants, we talk about deforestation and discuss that much of the world's original forests have been cut down.

Then we discuss the benefits of keeping old-growth forests and habitats alive. Here is a list of benefits my students and I have come up with:

- Plants can be used to make medicine.
- Forests provide intact ecosystems.
- Forests provide habitats.
- Forests create watersheds.
- Plants give off oxygen.
- Plants clean the air.
- Plants provide shade.
- Forests provide resources for local cultures.
- Plants improve aesthetics.

We discuss and elaborate on these benefits. I also share with my students the following anecdotes:

When trekking in the Himalayas, I was shocked to discover how much of their native forest had been stripped for the purpose of providing firewood for tourists. A local conservation group based in Katmandu is trying to educate the public with the hope of stopping the destruction. Unfortunately, Nepal has faced serious flooding and erosion during the past few years, and its reduced watershed is believed to have contributed to this. There is hardly any original forest left in Nepal.

In tropical Queensland, Australia, lies some of the most diverse rain forest in the world. It is estimated that there are more than two thousand species of plants in a single square mile of that forest! Many plants are still being discovered there. In the Queensland rain forest scientists are finding plants with medicinal values that may possibly cure cancer and other diseases.

My students and I conclude that it would be a tragedy to permanently lose any plant species.

Background Research on Plants

I ask my students to come up with a list of ten to twenty colorful or interesting plants in their parks. I have them focus their list on a variety of plant types, including flowers, bushes, and trees. Students can research five to ten of their plants by using encyclopedias and plant-identification booklets. Information the students should acquire on each plant includes the following items:

- its description
- how it reproduces
- what happens to the plant during each season: when it blooms, loses its leaves, and so on
- its habitat and biome
- what animals use the plant for food, housing, protection, and so on

Next, we call local nurseries to find out if the plants that are found in the students' parks are available by seed or seedling. I encourage each group of students to purchase and grow at least one of their park's plants in a small pot. Some seeds may need to be ordered, so it is important to introduce this project well ahead of time. During our national park fair, the student rangers display their plants with a poster illustrating and explaining the above information.

Plant-Identification Posters

Students can create Plant-Identification Posters on which plant parts are to be matched with pictures of their corresponding plants. The plant parts can include flowers, bark, needles, leaves, cones, and so on. The plant parts can be actual pieces taken from plants, which students might be able to obtain from a local plant nursery. Plant parts can be preserved by spraying them with hair spray or Spraylon, which is available in craft stores. If it is difficult to obtain enough plant parts to make a complete poster, sketches or pictures of the plant parts can be substituted.

Students first make rough sketches of their posters. Once I approve their designs, they can make their posters on poster board. On the right side of the poster, they attach pictures of the full plants. These pictures can be drawn or traced, or they can be actual photographs of the plants. Each plant is labeled. On the left side of the poster, they attach the plant parts in random order. Each plant part is labeled with the name of the plant, but these labels are covered with paper flaps.

When the posters are displayed, visitors can try to match the plant parts with their corresponding plants. They can check to see if they are correct by lifting the flaps below the plant parts.

Edible and Poisonous Plants Posters

I have my students create posters that show the edible and poisonous plants of their parks. First, I have my students look through the park information they received to find out which of the plants in their parks are edible and which are poisonous. They can also look through plant-identification books for this information.

Students then make an edible-plant poster of their park by illustrating and labeling each plant and noting where each plant is found in the park. They can create another poster with poisonous plants and include information about what the potential dangers of each plant are. During this activity, I always stress to students that they should *never* eat any plants in their parks, because they may misidentify a plant and because the parks don't allow visitors to pick the plants.

International Potluck

Once my students know some of the edible plants of their parks, we prepare a class international potluck, a project that is a good supplement to a study of foreign customs and cultures.

I ask my students to prepare food from the country in which their park is located. If possible, these dishes should include some sampling of plants or herbs—obtained from a grocery store or natural foods store—that grow naturally or are popular in the countries of the parks. The students can find recipes in international cookbooks. Once the students select their recipes, they prepare them at home as a homework assignment. Each dish should serve eight to ten students.

With all the sample dishes coming in, a full-course lunch consisting of world foods can be shared. During the potluck, I ask my student cooks to introduce their foods by talking about the origin of the food, the ingredients, and how they prepared it. At our national park fair, we give visitors food samples with accompanying recipe cards.

One of my favorite recipes that I have shared with my students is Dal-bhaat and Tarkari, which is a popular food I often ate while trekking through the Himalayas in Nepal. (See Figure 4–1 for the recipe.)

Ecosystem Murals

An ecosystem is a community of plants and animals that live together as a unit. Have students research the types of ecosystems—forest, desert, pond, marsh, and so on—that are located in their parks. Students choose one ecosystem and make a list of the plants and animals, including insects, that live in that environment. Students create a mural of their chosen ecosystems showing several of the plants, animals, and insects living in it. They'll need to include important information about the ecosystem by making illustrations that give hints showing food chains, animal behaviors, and their animals' lives during each season. These murals can be displayed in class. Important facts about the plants, animals, and insects can be written on index cards posted around the mural and connected to related pictures in the mural by strings of colored yarn.

Bark Displays

Have your students find out about the types of trees that are in their parks, where these trees are located, and what type of habitat they are in. After students have discovered information about the trees of their parks, they will need to also find out what the trees look like. Plant-identification books are a great resource for this research.

Students can then visit a local nursery to make a bark rubbing of one of the trees found in their parks, or one that is similar. If the nursery doesn't have a tree that is the same or similar to a tree found in a particular park, the student can draw or trace the bark pattern of the tree that is shown in a plant-identification book.

To make a bark rubbing, the student tapes white construction paper around the bark of the chosen tree. The student rubs a crayon of a color similar to that of the tree bark back and forth across the paper. He or she then cuts out the bark rubbing and attaches it to poster board. The poster can also include a sketch of the entire tree as well as information on the tree, including the size of the tree, its habi-

Dal-bhaat and Tarkari

(lentils and curried vegetables)

This recipe serves 4 people.

For the Dal:
- 2 tablespoons of cooking oil
- 1 onion, chopped
- 2 cloves of garlic, crushed
- ¼ teaspoon fresh ginger, grated
- ½ teaspoon turmeric
- 1 cup red lentils
- salt to taste

For the tarkari:
- 2 tablespoons of cooking oil
- ½ green chili, finely chopped (or ½ teaspoon chili powder)
- ¼ teaspoon fresh ginger, grated
- 1 teaspoon ground coriander
- 1 teaspoon ground cumin
- salt to taste
- 1 pound chopped mixed vegetables
  (potatoes, carrots, peas, etc., parboil any root vegetables)

1. For the dal, heat the oil in a saucepan. Sauté the onion for a few minutes followed by the garlic until both ingredients are soft but not browned. Then add the ginger and cook for a few minutes. Next, stir in the turmeric and lentils. Pour on enough water to cover the lentils. Cover the pot and bring to a boil. Reduce heat and simmer 20 minutes or until the lentils are soft and have absorbed most of the water. Salt to taste. Keep warm in a serving bowl.

2. Meanwhile, for the tarkari, heat the oil in a large pan. Add the chili (or chili powder), ginger, coriander, cumin, and salt. Sauté for a few minutes, stirring frequently. Add the vegetables and stir until they are well coated with the spices. Add a little water and cook 10 to 20 minutes, or until the vegetables are cooked.

3. Serve the lentils and vegetables in separate dishes with rice.

FIGURE 4–1: RECIPE FOR A POPULAR MEAL IN THE HIMALAYAS, MADE WITH EDIBLE PLANTS—HERBS—FROM THE AREA

tat, a list of animals that live near or in it, and uses of the tree in its native country.

Some of my students have made miniature copies of their bark rubbings to use as note cards.

5

Geography and Geology Projects

The World's Best Places lend them themselves naturally to various geography and geology projects, many of which will work with your science and social studies curricula. Geology specifically deals with the structure of the earth, while geography examines ways in which the earth's natural features affect human life and, in turn, the way human life affects the earth. In this chapter, you will learn how students can study the makeup and movement of glaciers; issues relating to watersheds of a particular area; what the threats are to the overall environment of a region; how to measure geologic time and how to create volcanic lava flow, as well as other information. When doing any of these demonstrations, safety is important; anything that involves glass, heat, sharp objects, or chemicals should only be done by adults or with adult supervision.

Visitor Information Projects

Before people visit any of the parks, they usually need to first find out about the park and the country in which it is located. They need to know about the climate, the terrain, accommodations, rules, the culture, and the plant and animal life, and how to be safe during their travels. A fun way to compile this information is to create Visitor Information Pamphlets and Travel Essentials Suitcases.

Visitor Information Pamphlets

Students create colorful pamphlets that include information that visitors to the park should know. Not only does this project support a science and social studies curriculum but it can also be an excellent language arts project.

The Visitor Information Pamphlets should have brief summaries of key information related to the park and should cover some of the following topics, as well as any others that are relevant to the park or your particular course of study.

- accommodations
- weather
- safety
- trails
- scenery that the area is know for
- animals
- plants
- country (regional information)
- local culture
- visa information
- vaccinations needed

Students search through all park information, tag relevant information, and then continue to summarize appropriate information on note cards. I always allow for some flexibility in pamphlet topics because some groups will find ample information and others may not. When the students think that they have enough information to start the pamphlets, they need to show me their note cards so I can see if they are ready to proceed.

When several groups are ready to start the rough drafts of their pamphlets, I demonstrate how to create a pamphlet. We get ideas by looking at some of the actual park pamphlets we have received, then I show them how to block out the pamphlet. The following are some key points I make in my demonstration.

- Use bullets to highlight information.
- Include pictures or art.
- Highlight key words.
- Block off sections.
- Use borders.
- Use color and variety.

The students create their rough drafts of the pamphlets on an 8½ X 11" sheet of paper, which they fold into thirds or some other way. Once I approve the drafts, the students can make their final pamphlets out of construction paper. They can also use a computer to put their final pamphlets together.

Travel Essentials Suitcase

A follow-up activity to Visitor Information Pamphlets is to have the students pack a Travel Essentials Suitcase with items a visitor would need for a trip to their park. For this project, I have my students thoroughly consider the area to which they are traveling. We think about such factors as the weather, season of travel, hazards, insects, altitude, culture, and foods. After finding the park information about these and other factors, students can pack an actual suitcase as if they were going to truly travel to the park. They can bring the suitcases from home, find them at thrift stores and yard sales, or make them from cardboard boxes decorated to look like suitcases.

A packing list should accompany the suitcase, for visitors to refer to as they look at the suitcase. The following are some items that can be included on the packing list.

- a list of vaccinations that are required or recommended
- food precautions (water filter, water purification tablets, giardia pills)
- first-aid kit and insect repellant(s)
- passport and visa
- travel books and brochures
- field guides and lists of dangerous plants and animals
- clothes
- umbrella, raincoat, sun hat, sunscreen
- binoculars, camera, and film
- information on currency exchange rates
- regional travel books

If you would like, you can include a whole lesson on currency exchange rates, since travelers going to parks in other countries would need to know this information. The exchange rates for different countries can be found by checking through local banks or looking on the Internet.

Glacier Projects

Many UNESCO reserves have active glaciers or have had glaciers as part of their geological history, including Yosemite National Park in California, Te Wahipounamu–South West New Zealand, Waterton Glacier International Peace Park of the United States and Canada, and Los Glaciares of Argentina.

A glacier is a large mass of ice and snow that moves slowly downhill. Two conditions must occur in order for glaciers to form: abundant amounts of snow must fall, and summertime temperatures must stay low enough so that snow remains on the ground throughout the year. When snow accumulates and compacts into ice, it becomes increasingly dense. When this dense ice accumulates to a depth of one hundred feet or more, the weight of the ice may initiate a downhill movement. At this point, an ice field becomes a glacier.

Glaciers move from a few inches up to a few feet or more each year, depending upon ice accumulation and the slope of the mountain. Glaciers continue to move as long as more snow falls on top of the glacier, then ice melts at the bottom. An advancing glacier is one that is growing and moving forward, and a retreating glacier is one that is losing size and moving backward. Crevasses are cracks that form in glaciers because of the movement of the glacier.

As glaciers move, they leave their mark by sculpting and grinding the land beneath them. One important change a glacier can make to a landscape is that it can eventually carve a V-shaped valley into a U-shaped valley because of the weight and movement of the glacial ice. Glaciers produce other types of spectacular scenery, including knife-edged ridges, pyramid peaks, polished basins called glacier cirques, and hanging canyons and valleys with cascades and waterfalls.

Glacial movement is powerful enough to polish the rock that the glacier moves across and to grind rock into fine powder called "glacial flour," which when exposed to sun emits an aqua-blue color in the water. Glacial movement also leaves behind erratics, which are rocks or boulders that a glacier has moved from one area to another, and moraines, which are piles of rock that the glacier pushes ahead as it advances.

Interesting examples of glaciers can be found in the Franz Josef and Fox Glaciers of UNESCO's Te Wahipounamu–South West New Zealand. The lower ends of these glaciers dip down to near sea level in temperate rain forests, where it seldom snows, because their upper ends lie in extremely high and snowy mountains so that the glaciers are quickly pushed downhill. These glaciers have classic glacial features including cracks; crevasses; ancient moraines, including some in the nearby ocean; and glacial flour in rivers below them. The glaciers are extremely active, which I know firsthand because I've personally witnessed them creaking and cracking.

When I introduce glaciers to my students, I show them geology books, magazines, and sources that have pictures of glaciers. We talk about what glaciers are, what creates them, and how they advance and retreat.

I tell my students that many places in the world were once covered with glaciers. I ask them what they think land that was formerly covered with glaciers might look like today. Then I show them pictures of places that once had glaciers, such as Yosemite National Park and the fjords of Norway. We compare these pictures to pictures of places that currently have glaciers, such as Alaska and Antarctica.

A good book about glaciers that you can share with your students is *Stickeen: John Muir and the Brave Little Dog* (1998, New York: Scholastic Inc.), which was written by one of the world's foremost pioneers on conservation, John Muir. Muir was intrigued by glaciers, and this book has some great tales about Muir and his dog exploring glaciers in Alaska.

The following are some glacier projects that I have used. These will work for any parks that have had or currently have glaciers.

Glacier Models

For this activity, students make models of how glaciers in their parks have changed over time. I came up with this activity when I was hiking along large glaciers in the Alps of Switzerland and noticed that the place I was hiking had markings showing the size of the glacier at different points in time; I was surprised at how small the glacier had become. Many glaciers across the globe are retreating rapidly now because of global warming.

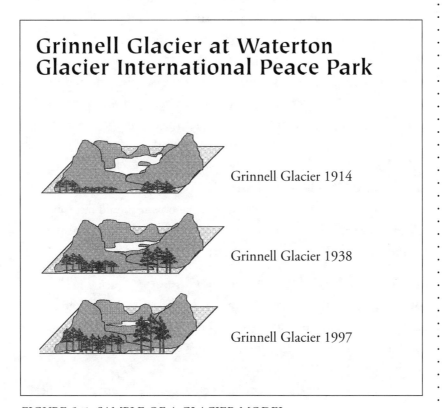

FIGURE 5–1: SAMPLE OF A GLACIER MODEL

Talk with your students about how and why glaciers advance and retreat. Then have your students research a glacier in their park to find out how it has advanced and retreated over a long period of time—fifty years or longer. They should also try to find a series of pictures or maps that illustrate the size of the glacier at several different points in time. Have them create three to four identical clay models formed to look like the terrain of their park where the glacier is located. On each clay model, they can press in a piece of white clay and shape it to indicate the size and location of the glacier for a specific time period. The students then set the series of clay models out in chronological order and label each model with the date and, if possible, the approximate size of the glacier on that date.

Your students can also try estimating the size of their glacier in the future. Have them create an additional clay model in their series and add a white clay glacier of whatever size they *predict* their glacier will be on some given date in the future.

The students can also create posters to go with their models, illustrating how the glaciers have changed over time, and they can create graphs that show the size of the glacier at different points of time, approximately every ten years.

Glacially Sculpted Rocks

This project shows how glaciers can polish and grind rocks. This project can either be demonstrated by you or student groups can do it themselves. Line a plastic or cardboard box that is approximately 12" square by 2" high with heavy aluminum foil. Pour a layer of fine sand and small pebbles into the box on top of the foil to represent the sand and rocks that are typically underneath glaciers. Pour water over the sand and rocks until the box is nearly full, and place the box in the freezer. When the water is frozen solid, remove the box from the freezer. Pull the block of ice from the box and set the box aside. Rub the ice block over clay or plasterboard to see how glaciers are able to scrape and polish rock surfaces. Examine the sand that remains in the box; it should feel rough. Show your students pictures of glacially sculpted rocks found at the parks; Yosemite National Park has excellent examples.

Landscape Features Created by Glaciers

With this activity, your students can see how glaciers can change the shape of landscapes by carving V-shaped valleys into U-shaped valleys and moving rocks to form moraines. They can also see how melting ice creates streams and waterfalls.

First, have your students make an oblong-shaped block of ice. The upper side of the ice block should be squared off while the bottom side

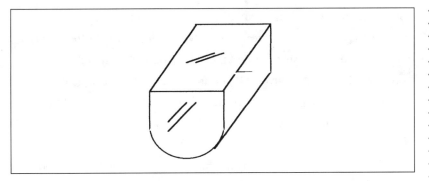

FIGURE 5–2: ICE BLOCK SHAPE FOR LARGE GLACIER

should be rounded into a hotdog shape (see Figure 5–2). To make the block of ice, in the bottom of a metal loaf pan or a plastic-lined shoe box, press ropes of clay along the longer sides near the bottom of the pan to create curved edges. Line the pan with heavy foil, fill the pan with water almost to the top, then set the pan in the freezer. At the same time, your students can also make ice cubes that can be used to represent smaller glaciers or icefields.

Meanwhile, in a school sandbox or in a large tub filled with sand, have your students create a sand mountain range, and shape one area into a V-shaped valley that is close to the size of the block of ice that was frozen. Have them add small rocks along the valley walls.

After the block of ice is frozen solid, have your students remove it from the pan or box and set it on the mountain just above the V-shaped valley they created in the sand. They can slowly push this "glacier" down the slope to see how glaciers push rocks and sand ahead of them to create moraines, then they can then set the block of ice in the V-shaped valley. The ice cubes can be placed about between the mountains.

Have your students observe the ice as it melts and creates streams and waterfalls. When the block of ice and ice cubes are fully melted, your students can see what land formations were created in the sand by their "glaciers." The V-shaped valley should have been reshaped into a U-shaped valley by the block of ice.

Students studying parks that have glaciers or that have had glaciers in the past can make posters that illustrate the land features created by the glaciers.

Geological History Time Line

Teaching geological history can be difficult. The length of time involved in the natural creation of the World's Best Places is a hard concept for students and most adults to comprehend. For example, there are rocks at the bottom of the Grand Canyon that are estimated to be more than forty million years old! In comparison, our life spans are a just a handful of decades. How can we as teachers convey geologic time? One way is with a Geological History Time Line. These time lines are one of the best ways I've discovered to give students an idea of the order of geological forces that have shaped the spectacular features in the World's Best Places.

I start by talking about Geological History Time Lines with my students and explaining what is included on them. Then I demonstrate how to create a time line by sketching an example on the chalkboard. I show my students how to use a ruler to mark off spaces for each event to illustrate how time has elapsed between one event and the next. For example, events that occurred close together in time would be set close together on the time line. I also show them how to alternate writing events above and below the time line in order to provide more space in which to write the information. A "break" in the time line, shown with two slash marks, is used to indicate that long periods of time have occurred between two events. We then talk about where to find the information that will be included on the time line, how to summarize it in a chronological list, and how to briefly write the event information, including dates, on the time line. As we talk, I have my students take notes on how to create the time lines.

Once my students understand how to create a geological history time line, I have them research information related to the geological history of their own parks and jot down all major geological events that have been given a specific time reference. They then list the events in order from the earliest to the most recent to create a chronological list (see Figure 5–3).

My students use the events they wrote on the chronological list to develop a rough-draft sketch of their time lines. Once students get approval from me on their drafts, they have a few options for completing their final time lines. One is to tape together several 11 x 17" pieces of construction paper on which to build their time lines. Another is to make the time line on poster board (see Figure 5–4). A third option, which is the most popular with my students, is to use a computer program that creates banners. I've had students build all or part of their time line using a computer. Finding a large enough space in which to display the banners can be a problem, but they can be displayed like a border around the classroom.

Other Geology and Geography Projects

Freezing Rocks

When water seeps into cracks in a rock and freezes, the water expands, splitting and eventually reshaping the rock. When this continues to happen over a long period of time, arches, pinnacles, bridges, and piles of

Chronological List for Yosemite National Park

- Sand, silt, and mud settle to ocean floor.
- Earth's forces shape rock into a mountain range.
- Molten rock forms beneath mountains.
- Weathering and erosion strip away sedimentary rock layer.
- Uplift continues; erosion increases because of steepness.
- Deep V-shaped canyons form.
- Upward-moving area ruptures; land to east settles to form a steep escarpment.
- Climate changes; large amounts of snow and ice accumulate.
- Glaciers form at Sierra Crest at least 3 different times.
- Glaciers move down steep river-carved canyons. Some glaciers in Yosemite become 3,000 feet deep.
- Glaciers polish rocks and carve scenery into U-shaped troughs and hanging valleys.
- Glaciers recede, leaving lakes behind.
- Lakes dry out to form meadows and forests.

FIGURE 5–3: SAMPLE CHRONOLOGICAL LIST

rock may form, creating the spectacular formations found in many World Heritage Parks.

Students can demonstrate the process of freezing and expanding in this activity. Have them fill a small jam jar with water and then screw on the lid. Place the jar in a clear plastic bag, tie the bag at the top, and put the bag in the freezer. After about twelve hours, remove the bag from the freezer and observe what has happened to the jam jar inside. The jar should have cracked because of the expansion of the frozen water.

I ask my students to imagine how this freezing and expansion process has shaped the rocks in their parks. They can draw a series of pictures on a poster to illustrate how the rocks were shaped. The posters can also show pictures of the spectacular rock features at their parks.

Hot Lava Demonstration

This activity is a teacher demonstration that illustrates a lava flow using candle wax. Many of the mountains around the world as well as those

Geological History Timeline for Yosemite National Park

470 TO 250 MYA
Deposition of sediment occurs.

80 MYA
First granite formations appear.

25 MYA TO NOW
Mountains uplift. Erosion forms canyons.

10,000 YA TO NOW
Glaciers recede. Lakes, meadows, forests remain.

NOW
Erosion and uplift continues. Domes exfoliate. A few very small glaciers remain.

225 TO 80 MYA
Sierra Nevada Mountain formation begins.

80 TO 25 MYA
Erosion begins.

2MYA TO 10,000 YA
Multiple glaciations occur.

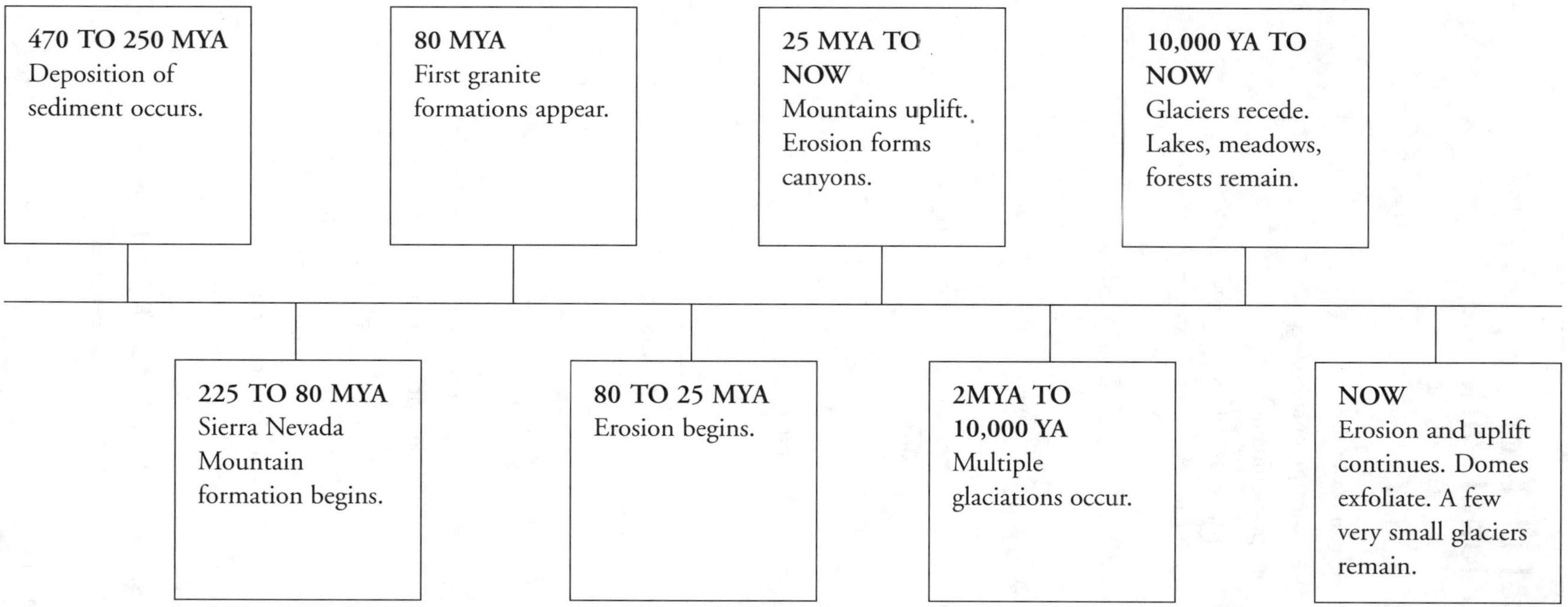

NOTE:
MYA: Million Years Ago
YA: Years Ago

FIGURE 5–4: SAMPLE GEOLOGICAL HISTORY TIME LINE FOR YOSEMITE NATIONAL PARK

located in the World Heritage Parks were shaped by volcanoes, many of which are still active. If there are volcanoes in a student's park, there are also recent and historical lava flows.

Fill a heat-tempered glass beaker with a mixture of equal parts of red unmelted candle wax, sand, and water. The mixture should come to within one centimeter of the top of the beaker. Set a Bunsen burner on a large sheet of heavy-duty aluminum foil. Use tongs to hold the beaker of wax mixture over the lighted Bunsen burner. Wear an oven mitt on the other hand for safety in case you need to hold the beaker. Your students can watch as the heated wax mixture oozes up over the surface of the beaker and flows over the sides, much like flowing lava. Talk about why the "lava" was able to flow after it was heated.

Allow the "lava" to cool and harden and talk with your students about why it no longer flows.

Lava Flow Demonstration

This is another lava flow activity you can demonstrate that shows how the distance over which lava flows varies with the temperature of the lava and the slope of the mountain down which the lava flows.

To represent the slope of a mountain, set one end of a wooden board on a stack of bricks so the board is at a forty-five-degree angle. Heat a red-colored jelly in a double boiler set on a burner until the jelly is hot enough to flow quickly. Warm a lighter-colored jelly by setting a jar of the jelly in a container of hot water. While your students watch, pour a bit of each type of jelly at the same time onto the upper part of the slope of the wooden board and watch them flow down. Then use a ruler to measure the distances each jelly flowed down the board. Talk with your students about why the hotter jelly traveled farther than the cooler jelly. Explain that in nature, lava flows more easily when it is hot and slows down as it becomes cooler. Once lava completely cools, it hardens and stays where it is.

Wipe off the board and set another brick under the end of the board to make the slope steeper. Pour both the jellies on the board and note the difference in the distance of each flow. Reduce the slope of the board until it is almost flat and repeat the activity. Talk with your students about why both jellies flowed farther on the steeper slope than they did on the flatter one.

When you have completed the lava activities, ask your students to picture the lava flows in their own parks. Have them create a map that illustrates where lava flow has occurred, and attach this map to a poster. The posters can also include information explaining the lava flow as it relates to temperature and slope.

Erosion Trays

With this activity, students see how water flowing across land can create different erosional features. This project has many variations, and it is one of the most exciting activities I've ever done with my students.

Tell your students that water flowing through rivers, streams, and waterfalls has helped to shape many of the features of all the parks. Provide a plastic tray or a plastic-lined wooden box that is approximately 24 x 24 x 5". On the bottom of the tray at one end there should be a drain hole through which water can flow out. Have the students fill the tray with soil, sand, or diatomaceous earth. Diatomaceous earth, a fine sandlike substance used in abrasives, polishes, and pool filters, works best and can be purchased from plant nurseries and pool supply stores. Elevate the end of the tray opposite the drain approximately five inches by setting it on a stack of books or boards. Place a shallow pan under the drain hole at the other end of the tray. The students can fill a pitcher with blue-colored water and slowly pour the water through a funnel or hose held over the soil at the elevated end of the tray. Then they can watch to see what erosional features are created, such as canyons, river valleys, alluvial fans, deltas, and plateaus. Waterfalls can also be created as water trickles downhill (see Figure 5–5).

The erosional features in the tray can be labeled using little flags made from toothpicks and strips of paper.

This activity can be varied by changing the slope of the tray, altering the topography, and adding plants and rocks. Students can also vary how the water is added to the box by doing such things as pouring in the water very quickly, pouring in a lot of water all at once, misting the soil with a spray bottle, and dripping water from an eyedropper.

Cave Formations

For this activity, your students can use papier-mâché to create three different types of cave formations: stalagmites, soda straws, and popcorn. To make the papier-mâché, use torn strips of newspaper moistened in a mixture of equal parts flour and water and a tiny bit of salt. Use the moistened papier-mâché strips to create the various cave formations described:

- **Stalagmites:** Stalagmites are cave formations shaped like cones that are built up on a cave floor. Have your students make very large stalagmites, up to eight feet tall, by shaping chicken wire into a cone shape. Empty, liter-size plastic bottles can be stuffed inside the chicken wire to help maintain the conical shape. Cover this shape with papier-mâché, and when it is thoroughly dry, spray paint with off-white paint.

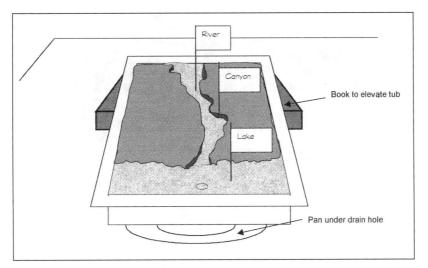

FIGURE 5–5: SAMPLE EROSION TRAY

- **Soda Straws:** Soda straws are small stalactites that hang from the ceiling of a cave. Have your students create them by covering regular drinking straws with papier-mâché. To make longer soda-straws, your students can tape together several drinking straws end-to-end. Once the papier-mâché dries, the soda straws can be painted off-white and hung from the ceiling.

- **Popcorn:** Popcorn is a type of cave formation that looks exactly like popcorn. To make popcorn, your students can simply put papier-mâché over actual pieces of popped popcorn. The papier-mâchéd popcorn pieces can be painted off-white or light brown and glued to the walls of your classroom.

Stalactites and Stalagmites

With this activity, you can show your class how stalactites and stalagmites are formed in caves. Fill two glass jars of the same size with warm water. Add a few tablespoons of baking soda to both jars and thoroughly stir. Continue adding soda to both jars until the soda no longer dissolves in the water. Cut one 24" strip of wool yarn. Tie a paper clip to both ends of the yarn. Place one of the paper clip ends of the yarn into each jar. Place a saucer between the two jars, positioning it below the yarn. Leave this set up for several days. Observe the yarn and the saucer. Stalactites should have formed on the yarn, and stalagmites should have formed in the saucer (see Figure 5–6).

Weathering Sandstone

Students can see how weathering affects sandstone with this activity. Weathering is the physical or chemical process that acts to break down rock and other materials. Physical weathering occurs when wind, water,

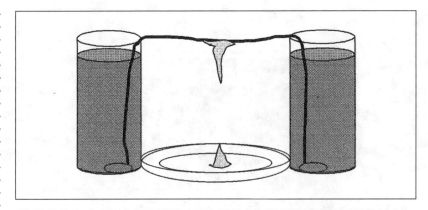

FIGURE 5–6: STALACTITE AND STALAGMITE FORMATION

and temperature changes break down rock into smaller particles without changing the minerals in the rock. Chemical weathering occurs when chemicals created from some types of acids break down rocks and change the minerals in the rocks.

Sandstone is a type of sedimentary rock made up of sand bonded together with natural cementing materials such as silica or iron oxide. Sandstone is often mixed with other rocks to create a conglomerate. Sandstone is a fairly soft stone and, therefore, it is highly erodable.

Many features in parks were shaped because of the weathering of sandstone. Arches, pillars, caves, and some canyons—like the Grand Canyon in Arizona—were created because sandstone was weathered.

For this project, have your students mix equal portions of powdered cement and water in a paper cup so that the cup is about half full. Have them stir some small pebbles into the cement mixture to create a conglomerate. After the cement hardens, they can peel away the paper cup. Cement hardens much like compressed sandstone does. Have your students examine the hardened cement and feel its texture. They can then imagine that their cement rock is sandstone found in nature. Have them describe what processes in nature might be able to weatherize and reshape the rock over time. Your students can then try various techniques to weatherize their cement rock, such as sanding it or shaking it repeatedly in a coffee can. They can also soak it in water for a period of time and freeze it for several weeks.

Your students can create posters illustrating the shaping of sandstone rocks within their parks. They can display their weathered cement rocks with their posters.

Super Erosion Chambers

For this group activity, students shake up a jar filled with sugar cubes to see how they erode. This is a great follow-up activity to the Weathering

Sandstone activity described previously.

Each student in a group of five students gets a sugar cube and uses a colored marker to color in all six sides of his or her cube. Everyone uses a different color for easier identification. The students put their colored sugar cubes together in one clear glass jar. Each student takes a turn shaking the jar ten to twenty times. When all students have had a turn, examine what is left of the sugar cubes. By looking at the colors on the sugar cubes, the students can see whose sugar cubes eroded the most from the shaking.

Wind Erosion

Erosion is the process through which land features are gradually worn away by the action of wind, water, glaciers, and waves. Wind can erode and shape large areas of land, especially when the wind is combined with the erosional effects of water and sloping topography. Wind erosion shapes rocks beautifully. Wind erosion can create caves, arches, pillars, and large sand dunes. If wind erosion has occurred in a student's park, it can be illustrated through this activity.

Have your students fill a tray with sand, rocks, and dirt. Elevate one end of the tray by setting it on a stack of books or boards. Hold a blow-dryer or fan over the sand mixture at the elevated end of the tray to show how wind erodes the sand. The students can vary this activity by raising and lowering the tilt of the tray, and they can also try adding water and plants to the sand. Your students can label the features created in their models, such as sand dunes, canyons, and mountains.

Metamorphic Rock Formations

Metamorphism, the changing of the shape and structure of rocks by heat, pressure, and water, happens continuously throughout the earth. Ask your students to find out if metamorphism is occurring in their preserves and what the visual effects are. They can demonstrate metamorphosis with this activity. Lay a large piece of heavy foil flat on a table. On the foil, lay a sheet of waxed paper. Bend a piece of 2 x 14" poster board into a circular column shape. Set the poster board column on top of the waxed paper. Inside the column of poster board, place enough broken crayons of various colors, with the paper wrappers removed, that they mound above the top edge of the column. The crayons represent rocks. Place another sheet of waxed paper on top of the cardboard column, then set an empty coffee can on top of this waxed paper. Be sure the coffee can is stable and that it is sitting on the mound of crayons and not resting on the poster board. Put an oven mitt on one hand and use that hand to hold the coffee can steady. With the other hand, slowly pour a pot of

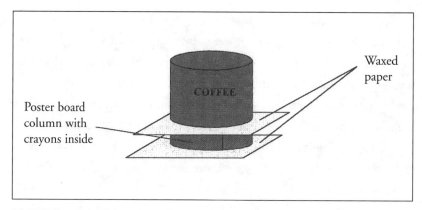

FIGURE 5–7: METAMORPHIC ROCK FORMATIONS

boiling water into the coffee can. Heat and pressure will force the crayons—the "rocks"—to melt into different shapes. This happens to various types of rocks when they are heated underground (see Figure 5–7).

Geysers

With this demonstration, you can show your students how geysers work. Geysers are spectacular natural occurrences. Yellowstone in the United States contains wonderful examples, as do many areas in New Zealand, including Tongariro. Volcanic areas have a variety of thermal features such as boiling pools, steam vents, fumaroles, bubbling mud pots, and geysers. If a student's park is volcanic in nature, there is a good chance it has numerous geysers. Have your students research the cause of geyser eruptions. They can find this information in websites on Yellowstone National Park, Tongariro National Park in New Zealand, and Iceland. Have them make posters illustrating the process.

Gather together a sixteen-ounce clear plastic juice bottle with a cap, a hammer, a nail, a thin straw, red food coloring, liquid dish soap, clay, a pot, a burner, and an oven mitt. Hammer a nail into the top of the bottle cap to make a hole that is just big enough for the thin straw to slide through; the hole should be tight enough to hold the straw in place. Fill the bottle with very warm tap water until the water is about one inch from the top. Add several drops of red food coloring and a tablespoon of liquid dish soap to the water. Snap the cap onto the bottle, then slide the straw through the hole in the cap until the straw reaches at least partway down into the water. Seal around the bottle cap with clay to keep air from getting into the bottle. Set the bottle aside. Fill the pot about three-fourths full with water. Place the pot on the burner, heat the water to a rapid boil, then remove the pot from the burner. Immediately put on an oven mitt and carefully lift the bottle into the pot. As you lift the bottle, be sure you do not squeeze it because the water may leak out of the straw. Hold the bottom of the bottle down in the pot of boiled water. Have your students gather around at a safe distance to watch, and make sure the top of the straw points away from your students and you. Within five minutes, colored water from inside the bottle should rise up into the straw and stream out of the top of the straw like a geyser.

You can repeat this activity and simulate steam vents, also called fumaroles. On either side of the straw opening, poke two pin holes through the clay and clear through the bottle cap. When you place the bottle in the hot water, steam should come out of the holes.

Researching Threats to the Health of UNESCO Reserves

Human activity changes and often endangers various features of the earth including land, water, and air. There are serious threats to UNESCO reserves all over the world. Some of these threats include the following:

- poaching
- mining
- deforestation
- diverted water supply
- pollution
- geothermal drilling
- overuse of cars and airplanes
- overcrowding
- wildlife trade

A few recent examples of specific problems in UNESCO reserves include the following:

- water diversion away from Florida's Everglades
- geothermal drilling outside of Yellowstone
- slaughter of migrating bison in Yellowstone
- boat overcrowding in Australia's Barrier Reef
- overuse of trees for trekker firewood near Sagarmatha in the Nepal Himalayas
- noise pollution from flights over the Grand Canyon
- poaching and deforestation in the Virunga/Kahuzi-Biega Gorilla Reserves in Zaire
- acid rain in the Great Smokies

Students need to know what threats their parks face and what can be done to stop the problems. I have my students write brief summaries on the threats to their parks. The students share these summaries with the class, then we learn about potential results of some of these threats through the following activities.

Forest Death

Trees all over the world are dying. Some of the more common causes of forest death are acid rain, smog, and logging. The Great Smokey Mountains, a UNESCO park, has had problems with acid rain, which is created when industrial waste is emitted into the air and later falls with rain. Sequoia trees in Yosemite National Park are being affected by smog from the nearby San Joaquin Valley. Have your students study the forests of their parks to see if they are being damaged in any way.

Students can also compare the forest death of their parks to any environmental damage that is happening in their state or local area. Students can find out if there is anything that can be done to prevent this forest death. I have the students make posters showing what is happening near where they live and/or in their park. Posters can also show what can be done to stop it.

A Tree Will Be Cut Down

The cutting of old-growth trees is controversial. Recently in Redwood National Park, a World Heritage Park in Northern California, a woman named Julia Hill climbed down from an old-growth tree that she had lived in for two years to protest the cutting of that and other trees. Once on the ground, she said to reporters, "My hope is that the lumber companies do things differently and embrace sustainable logging practices, forswearing clear-cuts that cause mudslides when it rains" (Eric Brazil, "'Butterfly' Descends from Tree," *San Francisco Chronicle,* Dec. 19, 1999, C–1, C–8).

I have my students study the ecosystems and habitats in their parks until I feel that they know their park's natural features and wildlife and they understand how the two are interconnected. Then, I tell them to imagine that an old-growth tree is going to be cut down in their park. Students write three to five paragraphs from different points of view related to the tree being cut down. Points of view might include a bird, a snake, a deer, a logger, a ranger, a visitor, an environmentalist, a news reporter, or others. These paragraphs can be displayed in class. A picture or poster can accompany the paragraph. This is an excellent language arts project. A great follow-up activity is reading the books *The Giving Tree* by Shel Silverstein and *The Lorax* by Dr. Seuss.

Damaged Watersheds

This activity shows students how a damaged watershed outside their park can lead to problems within their park. A watershed is the ridge

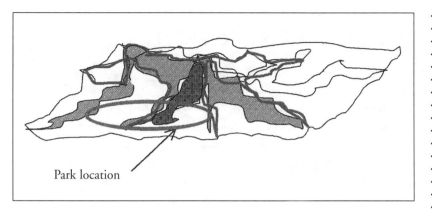

Park location

FIGURE 5–8: CRUMPLED WATERSHED PAPER

between areas that are drained by two different rivers or streams. Forests and natural vegetation are vital to watersheds because they keep water from flowing too quickly down the hillsides and causing erosion, flooding, silted water, and damaged fisheries. Therefore, when land is heavily logged, the area's watershed can also be destroyed.

UNESCO national parks are like islands of refuge, protecting the last of a habitat, its species, and its watershed. However, near the borders of some national parks, including Olympic National Park in Washington and Redwood National Park in California, extensive logging has led to erosion and flooding, causing silted water to ruin salmon spawning grounds inside the parks. As a local logger said to Julia Hill after her two-year tree sit, "You probably saved our lives because the land above our homes would have collapsed if it had been logged" (Eric Brazil, "'Butterfly' Descends from Tree," *San Francisco Chronicle,* Dec. 19, 1999, C–1, C–8).

For this activity, each student has a sheet of white 8½ x 11" paper. Near one of the paper's edges, they can use a brown watercolor marker to draw in a 1½" diameter circle. This circle represents their park. Have them crumple up the paper then open it back up and slightly flatten it out with the side with the park drawn on it facing up. The peaks in the paper represent actual mountains near their parks, while the lower areas represent actual valleys and low-lying regions. The students color the tops of the ridges and peaks with blue watercolor markers to represent the start of the watersheds. On several raised areas near their parks, color the "mountainsides" with black watercolor marker to represent areas that have been heavily forested (see Figure 5–8).

Place the crumpled paper on a sheet of newspaper. Hold an eye-dropped filled with water over the ridges and peaks and squeeze the pipette so that a steady stream of water flows from it onto the paper. The blue-colored water flowing down the raised areas represents the

Tongariro Creation Story

The most popular Maori legend about Tongariro is that there were once more than three mountains in the park. The mountains were all in love with the womanly Mount Pihahoa to the north. The mountains fought and the losers vanished, but they could only do so in the darkness of night. The mountains that remain in the North Island is where daylight touched them.

The volcanic fires of Tongariro were kindled when the priest and explorer Ngatoro-i-rangi was in danger of freezing to death on the mountains. His prayers for assistance were answered by the fire demons of Hawaii who sent fire by way of White Island and Rotorua to burst through the mountaintops. To appease the gods, Ngatoro cast his female slave, Ngauruhoe, into the volcano. The then unnamed crater took its name from her.

FIGURE 5–9: TONGARIRO CREATION STORY

flowing water of the watersheds. Black-colored water represents mudslides and silted floodwaters flowing downhill. Refill the pipette and continue to drip water on the ridges and peaks. Ask your students to observe what happens within the borders of their parks.

I have my students make posters illustrating their parks' watershed, including the water cycle. The posters include locations where the rain (or snow) typically falls, the rivers and streams of the watershed areas, ponds and lakes, villages in and around the park, and the forests.

After researching to find out how damaged watersheds have affected areas around their parks, the students can make another poster showing a similar landscape with forests that have been logged. This poster could show the results of overlogging.

Park Creation Legends

Through the geography and geology projects, my students just begin to discover the World's Best Places. Most of what they have learned about the creation of their parks is from the teachings of modern science. However, for thousands of years, local and indigenous cultures have had their own stories that explain the creation of these special places, which students should also consider when studying their parks (see Figure 5–9).

After reading the passage about the creation of Tongariro to my class, I talk about the volcanic features of Tongariro. My students and I compare the Tongariro creation story to how modern science would explain its creation.

I have my students look through their park information for creation legends on their own parks. Then they prepare oral presentations of their legends. First, I have the student groups read their creation legends out loud within their groups for practice. They next decide on their favorite way to present their creation legends to an audience; it can be through readers theater, plays or skits, choral readings, flannel board stories, or many other ways. I allow my students to elaborate on their stories if necessary to create scripts. An added project choice for this activity would be for the students to create props and costumes to use during the presentation. The students spend time rehearsing for their presentations, which can be made not only to their class but to other classes as well.

Appendix A: Park Descriptions

· ·

CONTENTS

As of December 1999, UNESCO had designated 630 World Heritage Sites around the world. Four hundred eighty of the sites are cultural, 128 are natural, and 22 are mixed. I selected thirty-two of these World Heritage Sites for inclusion in this book (See Figure A–1 on page 71).

I selected these thirty-two sites for several reasons. First, they represent a variety of locations worldwide, which promotes exposure to different countries, climates, biomes, topography, and cultures. Second, these sites are generally well-known worldwide, so information about the sites is more readily available than it would be for lesser-known places. Finally, they represent what I think are the most popular attractions and ones that students will most eagerly study and remember.

Lists of the World Heritage Parks and information on individual parks, including the thirty-two parks included in this book, can be found at this UNESCO Internet address: *http://www.unesco.org/whc/nwhc/pages/sites/main.htm*. At this site, you can click on "World/Country/Detail Maps" to get the full worldwide list of parks or click on "Inscribed Sites" to get park lists by region. If you click on any of the park names on the lists, you will be shown detailed information about that particular park, including addresses and phone numbers you can use to get more information. There is also a list of sites in danger.

In addition to the UNESCO website, you can find information about national parks of North America at this Internet address: *http://www.national-park.com*. You can also type in the individual park names and the countries they're in as keywords in order to locate additional information on the Internet.

Brief summaries of all thirty-two sites, arranged by continent, follow.

North America

United States
Everglades National Park

Everglades National Park
40001 State Road 9336
Homestead, Florida 33034-6733
Phone: (305) 242-7700

The Everglades is one of the most diverse and most threatened ecosystems on the planet. The Everglades is actually a wide, flat river that begins in Lake Okeechobee and ends at the Gulf of Mexico. The Everglades represents the largest continuous stand of saw grass prairie left in North America, as well as the largest mangrove ecosystem in the

The World's Best Places

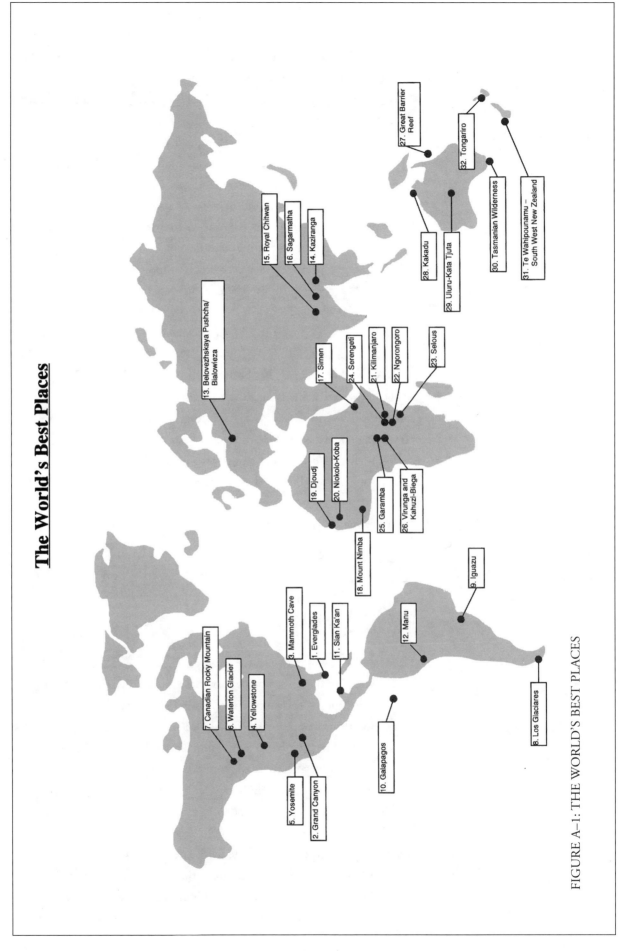

FIGURE A–1: THE WORLD'S BEST PLACES

1. Everglades
2. Grand Canyon
3. Mammoth Cave
4. Yellowstone
5. Yosemite
6. Waterton Glacier
7. Canadian Rocky Mountain
8. Los Glaciares
9. Iguazu
10. Galapagos
11. Sian Ka'an
12. Manu
13. Belovezhskaya Pushcha/ Bialowieza
14. Kaziranga
15. Royal Chitwan
16. Sagarmatha
17. Simen
18. Mount Nimba
19. Djoudj
20. Niokolo-Koba
21. Kilimanjaro
22. Ngorongoro
23. Selous
24. Serengeti
25. Garamba
26. Virunga and Kahuzi-Biega
27. Great Barrier Reef
28. Kakadu
29. Uluru-Kata Tjuta
30. Tasmanian Wilderness
31. Te Wahipounamu – South West New Zealand
32. Tongariro

Western Hemisphere. Indigenous cultures have lived in and around the Everglades for hundreds of years. First preserved as a national park in 1947, the Everglades is now a World Heritage Site and an International Biosphere Reserve.

The park has a unique mix of tropical and temperate plants and animals. Small bands of trees known as hammocks support tropical plants such as orchids, ferns, palms, and gumbo-limbo. There are also swamp forests, pine forests, and mangrove swamps. Perhaps best known for its bird life, the Everglades is home to an extensive list of rare birds. Mammals include the opossum, raccoon, fox, otter, deer, black bear, and extremely rare Florida panther. Manatees, porpoises, turtles, snakes, alligators, and crocodiles also live there. Many rare species in the Everglades are threatened and endangered, including the Florida panther, West Indian manatee, green sea turtle, American alligator, indigo snake, and southern bald eagle.

As southern Florida has been built up, water from the Everglades has been diverted away from the park. This has seriously affected plant and animal life in the glades. Steps to restore essential water flow are now being taken.

The Everglades offers rich opportunities for students to participate in the plant life, wildlife, and geography projects in this book.

Grand Canyon National Park

Grand Canyon National Park
PO Box 129
Grand Canyon, Arizona 82026
Phone: (520) 638-7888

The Grand Canyon is one of the largest and deepest canyons in the world. The Grand Canyon was cut by the Colorado River. The canyon bottom has exposed rocks up to forty million years old, which are some of the oldest rocks on Earth. Artifacts and remains of indigenous cultures are found in the park. The Grand Canyon has a varied plant life that ranges from dry desert at the canyon bottom to deep forests on the rim above. Desert plants include cacti and yuccas, and forest plants include aspens, spruces, and Ponderosa pines. The abundant wildlife includes coyotes, mountain lions, mule deer, snakes and lizards, and the endemic Kaibab squirrel. The squawfish and bald eagle are endangered and threatened animals. Pollution from the Los Angeles area in Southern California is reducing visibility in the Grand Canyon.

The Grand Canyon is a haven for student geologists who want to learn more through the geology projects in this book. Endangered and threatened species are also good topics for study.

Mammoth Cave National Park

Mammoth Cave National Park
Mammoth Cave, Kentucky 42259
Phone: (502) 758-2328

With more than 350 miles of mapped passages, Mammoth Cave is the world's longest cave system. It is over three times longer than any other known cave. Although much of the system is mapped, geologists estimate that many more unmapped areas exist in the cave. There is extensive human history in and around the caves. Evidence shows that more than four thousand years ago, indigenous cultures mined the caves. In recent years, Mammoth Cave has been used for mining saltpeter for gunpowder, as an underground chapel for weddings, and as a hospital ward for those with tuberculosis. Since 1816, the caves have been a highly popular tourist destination; today, spelunking tours, historic tours, and tours by boat are offered.

Above the caves, the rolling hillsides are covered with sinkholes where the caves' roofs have collapsed. Forested areas of the park have hickories, oaks, ashes, elms, sycamores, and maple trees. Wildlife includes the fox, beaver, coyote, mink, bobcat, deer, wild turkey, and a large variety of snakes and turtles. Living within the caves are blind shrimp, cave fish, spiders, mites, beetles, and salamanders. The pink pearly mussel, the Kentucky shrimp, the Indian bat, and the gray bat are among the endangered species in the park. Acid rain from pollution may be causing problems to the groundwater supply and it eventually might affect the caves and the wildlife dwelling within them.

Encourage your students to try geology projects as well as wildlife and geography projects when studying this park.

Yellowstone National Park

Yellowstone National Park
National Park Service Information Office
PO Box 168
Yellowstone National Park, Wyoming 82190
Phone: (307) 344-7381

Yellowstone National Park is the world's first national park. It became a preserved area in 1872. It is best known for its geothermal features. The entire Yellowstone basin is in a caldera, or collapsed volcanic zone. It has more concentrated geothermal features than any other place in the world. There are geysers, fumaroles, boiling lakes, and mud and steam vents. Old Faithful is the best-known geyser. Yellowstone has many lakes, waterfalls, and wild rivers. The lodgepole pine is Yellowstone's most common tree, and other trees include aspens and the Ponderosa pine. Mammals living in the park include the coyote, mountain lion, bighorn sheep, mule deer, pronghorn antelope, elk, moose, black bear, and one of the last remaining herds of wild bison. The grizzly bear is one of the park's threatened species, and gray wolves were just reintroduced in the park.

Many critical issues affect Yellowstone National Park. Mining and foresting at the borders of the park are reducing wildlife within the park. Recently, hundreds of bison were killed as they were migrating out of the park in the winter. Potential geothermal drilling could dry up the geysers.

To help students understand the geyser threat, try the geyser project in this book. Also, try some of the projects that address human impact on the environment.

Yosemite National Park

Yosemite National Park
PO Box 577
Yosemite National Park, California 95389–0577
Phone: (209) 372-0200

Yosemite National Park is known for its dramatic granite cliffs and towering waterfalls. The park also has U-shaped and hanging valleys, towering peaks, and high mountain meadows. John Muir, the world's most famous environmentalist, came to the park in the early 1900s and discovered extensive evidence of glaciation. Granite monoliths like Half Dome and El Capitan were literally cut by glaciers; now only a few small glaciers remain in the high country. The extensive history of glaciation and the powerful scenery left behind make Yosemite an incredible school of natural history. Yosemite National Park is home to the world's largest tree, the giant sequoia. Other trees include pines, firs, aspens, oaks, maples, and cedars. Yosemite has abundant mule deer, black bear, and coyote populations. Some of the many other animals are the river otter, weasel, porcupine, marmot, ringtail, badger, skunk, raccoon, bobcat, and bighorn sheep.

The winter of 1996–1997 brought devastating floods to Yosemite Valley, and the park will not be repairing many of the flood-damaged roads, buildings, and campgrounds. As Yosemite has been overwhelmed with tourists over the years, many people hope the lack of repairs will encourage tourists to stay away from the park.

Yosemite's geologic history makes it a good park for the study of glaciers and their effects. Students will also enjoy doing any of the plant life projects on the giant sequoia.

United States and Canada

Waterton Glacier International Peace Park

Waterton Lakes National Park
Waterton Park, Alberta, Canada T0K 2M0
Phone: (430) 859-2224

Glacier National Park
National Park Service
PO Box 128
West Glacier, Montana 59936
Phone: (406) 888-7800

Waterton Glacier International Peace Park is a land of high mountains, deep U-shaped valleys, alpine meadows, dense forests, and prairie grasslands. Glacier National Park has a unique combination of ecosystems, wildlife, and habitats. It is one of the most ecologically intact areas remaining in temperate regions of the world. Glacier and the adjoining Waterton Lakes National Park across the Canadian border form the Glacier–Waterton park system, the world's first international peace park.

In 1932, Glacier became protected as a national park, and Waterton Glacier International Peace Park was designated a World Heritage Site in 1995.

Ancient cultures hunted buffalo in the area and fished the lakes. Blackfoot Indians controlled the land in the eighteenth and nineteenth centuries.

Evidence of glaciation is everywhere in the park. There are deep U-shaped valleys, knife-edged ridges, hanging valleys, and lakes colored turquoise because of the grinding of rocks by glaciers above the lake. It has one of the few triple divides in the world, with water flowing to the Atlantic, Pacific, and Arctic Oceans. There are forty-eight small glaciers, thirty-five of which are named, that are still active in the park. These glaciers are shrinking, and evidence suggests that at the current rate of melting, they will all be gone in about thirty years.

Waterton Glacier International Peace Park has an abundance of wildflowers, especially in the high mountain meadows during summer. Bear grass lily is the official park flower. Trees include the western hemlock, western red cedar, Douglas fir, lodgepole pine, Englemann spruce, and subalpine fir.

Many large mammals live in the park, including grizzly bears, black bears, elk, moose, gray wolves (which recently migrated to the park), mountain goats, and bighorn sheep. Endangered species are the grizzly bear, wolf, bald eagle, and peregrine falcon. Recently, the park has tried to manage bear encounters and related problems through the use of guard dogs in selected campgrounds.

This park offers many opportunities for your students to study glaciers as well as plant life, wildlife, geology, geography, and some ancient cultures.

Canada

Canadian Rocky Mountain Parks

Banff National Park
PO Box 900
Banff, Alberta, Canada T0L 0C0
Phone: (403) 762-1550

Jasper National Park
PO Box 10
Jasper, Alberta, Canada T0E 1E0
Phone: (780) 852-6176

Kootenay National Park
PO Box 220
Radium Hot Springs, British Columbia, Canada V0A 1M0
Phone: (250) 347-9615

Yoho National Park
PO Box 99
Field, British Columbia, Canada V0A 1G0
Phone: (250) 343-6783

The Canadian Rocky Mountain Parks encompass Banff, Jasper, Kootenay, and Yoho National Parks. There are two million preserved acres of magnificent Canadian Rocky Mountain scenery with jagged peaks, U-shaped valleys, deep canyons, glaciers, waterfalls, rivers, lakes, bogs, and forests. Up to an elevation of two thousand meters are coniferous forests, with lodgepole pines, Douglas firs, and white spruces on lower slopes, and Englemann spruces, alpine firs, birches, and aspens above. Tundra occurs above 2,200 meters. There are more than five hundred species of flowering plants, including columbines, heaths, and heathers. Amongst the many mammals in the Canadian Rocky Mountains are wolves, mountain goats, bighorn sheep, deer, elk, moose, caribou, and black bears and grizzly bears. Chickadees, wrens, thrushes, mallards, ptarmigans, Canada geese, and golden and bald eagles are some of the two hundred species of birds that live there. In the Canadian Rocky Mountains, winters are long and cold and summers are short. The heaviest precipitation, which is mostly snowfall, occurs on the western slopes.

The Canadian Rocky Mountain Parks offer students the opportunity to study plant life, wildlife, geology, and geography; try any of these projects in this book.

South and Central America

Argentina

Los Glaciares

Intendencia, Parque Nacional Los Glaciares
Avda. del Liberator 1302
El Calafate (9405)
Provincia de Santa Cruz
Phone: 54-902-91005

In the Andes Mountains of southwestern Argentina is Los Glaciares, a spectacular subantarctic landscape of lakes, mountains, large glaciers, and eternal snows. In the park is the thirty-three-mile-long Moreno Glacier, which stretches down to Lake Argentino, where chunks of glacial ice carve into the lake. Eight major glaciers make up the Southern Patagonian Ice Field, which is the largest sheet of ice in the Southern Hemisphere outside of Antarctica. There are numerous mountains more than three thousand meters high, which were formed by uplift, volcanoes, and glacial erosion. Mammals that inhabit Los Glaciares include the chinchilla, pudu (the world's smallest deer), guanaco, huemal, cougar, gray fox, and armadillo. There are parakeets, sparrows, swans, eagles, rheas, and condors, as well as several species of fish, including the poisonous snouted lancehead fish. Severe weather occurs here, including rain, sleet, snow, and strong winds.

Students will enjoy studying the glaciers and climate of this park.

Argentina and Brazil

Iguazu National Park

Intendencia Parque Nacional Iguazú
Avda. Victoria Aguirre 66
cp 3370
Puerto Iguazú, Misiones
Phone: 54 757 20722

The central feature of the Iguazu is a two-mile-wide river waterfall. The Rio Iguazu passes through a basalt plateau, and where the volcanic rock abruptly stops, the river plunges over the edge, creating the world's widest waterfall. The waterfall creates a perpetual mist that prompts locals to call it "Where the clouds are born." In this park are tropical rain forests with more than two thousand recorded plant species, including orchids, vines, bamboo, and palms. Amongst the more than four hundred bird species are hummingbirds, parakeets, swifts, rufous oven-birds, woodpeckers, toucans, parrots, and trogons. There are also monkeys, caimans, coatis, tapirs, raccoons, sloth bears, anteaters, pumas, jaguars, and armadillos. Countless insects inhabit the Iguazu, along with twenty different species of butterflies. The Iguazu area, which was discovered by the Spanish in 1541, has been a sacred burial place for the Tupe-Guarani-Paraguas tribes for thousands of years.

Students will enjoy studying the exotic plant life and wildlife in this park.

Ecuador

Galapagos National Park

Superintendenta, Servicio Parque Nacional Galapagos
Puerto Ayora
Isla Santa Cruz
Phone (Darwin Research Station): 593-5-526-146

The Galapagos, which were discovered by the Spanish in 1535, are comprised of thirteen main islands and several smaller islands. They are located on the equator, one thousand kilometers west of Ecuador. The islands are considered to exhibit some of the world's best examples of evolution. Charles Darwin studied there in the 1800s, and frequent scientific research excursions continue today. These volcanic islands were colonized by chance migrants that either flew, floated, or swam the six huundred-mile distance from the mainland of South America. Once there, because of isolation, they adapted to the distinct conditions of each island. The Galapagos have beautiful beaches, lava caves called "tubes," boiling lakes, ancient lava flows, and great snorkeling areas. Plants include ferns, cacti, thickets, and mangroves. There is an incredible wildlife display with geckos, lava lizards, marine iguanas, sea lions, giant tortoises, and Sally light-footed crabs. Blue-footed boobies, mockingbirds, penguins, Darwin's finches, flamingos, pelicans, and herons are some of the birds that live there. At the lower elevations, the climate is dry and tropical, and at the higher levels, it is more moist.

Try some of the plant life and wildlife projects, along with the projects on volcanoes. Have students do some background research on Charles Darwin.

Mexico

Sian Ka'an

Secretaria de Medio Ambiente
Recursos Naturales y Pesca
Direccion de la Reserve de la Biosfera de Sian Ka'an
Avda. Insurgentes s/n, entre au.
Tec. de Merida y av. Tec. de Chetumal
Quintana Roo, Mexico C.P. 77039
Phone: (983) 228-29/200-73

In the state of Quintana Roo on the Yucatan Peninsula is Sian Ka'an, with coral reefs, exotic marine habitats, lagoons, wetlands, and forests. Sian Ka'an means "origin of the sky" in Mayan. For hundreds of years, the area was inhabited by the Mayans, and there are many Mayan ruins and archaeological sites within the reserve. One-third of the park is tropical forest, one-third is wetlands, and the remaining third is marine. Sian Ka'an is home to the world's second-largest barrier reef, the Gama Reef, which is a popular snorkeling site. The keys and bays are nesting sites for thousands of water birds. More than 350 species of birds are found in the park, including egrets, belted kingfishers, frigate birds, blue herons, boat-billed herons, and jabiru storks. Mammals include crocodiles, monkeys, ocelots, pumas, and jaguars. Amongst the marine life are tropical fish and endangered sea turtles, which nest on the beaches.

Have your students participate in projects that explore each of the different types of environments of the park: tropical forest, wetlands, and marine.

Peru

Manu National Park

Manu National Park
Heladeros 157 of .34
Apartado 1057
Cuzco, Peru

Manu National Park may be the only accessible piece of virgin rain forest left in the world. The park was originally protected in 1973, and the land size was later increased to create a total reserve. Much of the park is still unexplored. In Manu, there are cultural zones, where people can live and farm, and there are reserve zones, where people can study the area and tour the region. Tours are offered only by boat. Indigenous peoples, rangers, and scientists live in the park, but no missionaries are allowed. The park encompasses the Manu River watershed as it drops from its four-thousand-meter elevation in the Andes. There is dry grass above the tree line, a cloud forest with orchids and ferns below that, and lower still is a rain forest. This is an incredible, totally intact ecosystem with spider monkeys, tamarins, caimans, jaguars, otters, piranhas, and turtles. With more than one thousand species of birds, including parakeets, parrots, herons, and macaws, Manu is home to one-fifth of all Amazonian bird species.

Manu National Park is a wonderful place for students to try projects related to an entire ecosystem.

Europe

Poland and Belarus

Belovezhskaya Pushcha/Bialowieza Forest

Belovezhskaya Pushcha National Park
Settlement Kamenyuki
Kamenets District
Brest Region 225 063
Republic of Belarus
Phone: (016-31) 56-122

Bialowieza is Poland's oldest national park and was founded in 1921. Polish kings once owned land in this park. There is a total of sixty-two species of mammals living in the park, including tarpans (European wild horses), stags, roe deer, wild boars, lynx, wolves, moose, elk, and beavers. It is also a breeding center and reintroduction ground for the European bison. Capercaillie, black storks, eagles, and owls are amongst the many birds living in the park's forests. Oak, hornbeam, linden, ash, maple, elm, and spruce are some of the trees. Bialowieza contains the largest remaining virgin forest on the central European plains; some trees are up to four hundred years old. The park terrain is mostly lowlands and marshes. The mean annual temperature is seven degrees Celsius, and the annual precipitation, which is mostly composed of snow, is 612 millimeters.

Have your students participate in wildlife projects, obtaining what information they can about the reintroduction of a species. Also, have them try plant life projects that focus on the park's virgin forest.

Asia

India

Kaziranga National Park

Director
Kaziranga National Park
PO Bokakhat
District Jorhat
Assam 785 612

Kaziranga is home to the endangered one-horned rhinoceros, which has been hunted nearly to extinction. Located between the Himalayas, the park is a wide, open river valley of grassland that is ideal for wildlife viewing. Elephant grass grows up to six meters high, and there are swamps and pools covered with hyacinths and gallery forests full of acacias. Inhabiting the Kaziranga are many mammals, including monkeys, sloth bears, tigers, leopards, elephants, water buffalo, and the almost-extinct pygmy hog. Amongst the birds are partridge, egrets, storks, darters, fishing eagles, herons, and gray pelicans. One type of bird, the cattle egret, lives on rhinoceroses, eating the bugs that are on the skin of the rhino. It rains during Kaziranga's hot season, and the cool months are December and January.

The rich diversity of wildlife and plant life in Kaziranga National Park makes it an excellent choice for the wildlife and plant life projects described in this book.

Nepal

Royal Chitwan National Park

Chief Warden
Chitwan National Park Headquarters
Kasra Durbar
Narayani Zone

Situated at the foothills of the Himalayas and overlooking the Ganges
Plain are a series of transverse valleys between the Rapti and Rue Rivers.
Within the valleys, on an alluvial fan formed by river sedimentation
from the Himalayas, is Royal Chitwan National Park. Within the seasonal swamps and marshes of the park live the very rare Indian rhinoter-
os, as well as nilgais, wild boars, sloths, deer, hyenas, leopards, elephants,
and Bengal tigers. The park has recovery programs for the Gangetic dol-
phin and also gharials and marsh crocodiles. With more than four hundred species, bird life is prolific and includes pintails, partridge, egrets,
ibis, storks, herons, vultures, and eagles. The plant life primarily consists
of tall grasses in swamps, reeds and grasses in savannas, dense thickets
along rivers, and forests in the hill regions. Indigenous peoples also live
within the park. The weather remains cold from November through
April, and during the rainy season between June and September there is
typically flooding.

Royal Chitwan National Park presents good opportunities for geology and geography projects, as well as projects involving endangered and
reintroduced species.

Sagarmatha National Park (including Mount Everest)

Warden
Sagarmatha National Park Headquarters
Namche Bazar
Solu-Khumbu District
Sagarmatha Zone

Within Sagarmatha Park is Mount Everest, which, at more than 8,848
meters (approximately 28,000 feet), is the world's tallest mountain.
Many other high peaks, as well as numerous glaciers and icy rivers, lie
within the boundaries of the park. People come from all over the world
to climb Mount Everest and the surrounding peaks. Sagarmatha is home
to Nepal's Sherpas, who came from Tibet in the 1530s, about four hun-

dred years ago, during the Chinese occupation, and monasteries and tiny villages dot the hills. Red pandas, snow leopards, antelope, black bucks, buffalo, and elephants live in the park. Amongst the birds are snow pigeons, snow partridge, pheasant, and golden eagles. Various life zones exist within Sagarmatha Park. At lower elevations are tropical deciduous forests. Next are subtropical wet hill forests and above that are temperate-moist montane forests with orchids, rhododendrons, oaks, and conifers. In the subalpine zone are wildflowers, dwarf rhododendrons, junipers, and birches. Depending upon the altitude, the climate of Sagarmatha varies from tropical to tundra.

Sagarmatha is a wonderful place for all kinds of study, especially geology, because the park contains Mount Everest as well as other mountains in the Himalayas—the only mountain range on Earth that is still growing taller.

Africa

Ethiopia

Simen National Park

Chief Park Warden
Simen Mountains National Park
Debär, Gondar

Simen is a forest reserve with spectacular beauty. Located on the slopes of the Mount Wochocha Volcano at elevations between 2,400 and 3,425 meters, it is a protected mountain habitat of virgin forests. The climate is temperate to 2,600 meters, and it is generally cold and dry at higher elevations. The rainy seasons of Simen are during March and April and June through September. There are horizontal vegetation zones around the volcano: on the lower belts are eucalypt plantations, on the middle belts are cedar and podocarpus, and on the higher belts are kussotrees and heath trees. The park also has savannas and cultivated areas. The volcano's lava and sandstone have heavily eroded, creating deep stream-carved gorges. Amongst the mammals found in Simen are guereza, vervets, Simen foxes, gelada baboons, black bushbucks, duikers, caracals, leopards, wildcats, baboons, and ibexes. The most famous birds of the park are the white-cheeked touraco and the rare lummergeyer.

Simen's volcano offers students the chance to try projects involving volcanic activity; students can also be encouraged to research the park's unusual vegetation and wildlife.

Guinea and Ivory Coast

Mount Nimba Strict Nature Reserve

Station Biologique des Monts Nimba
S/X INRDG, BP 561
Conakry

Originally established in 1944, Mount Nimba Reserve protects an isolated mountain range and its surrounding peneplain. The mountain range is 1,200 meters high, 40 kilometers long, and 12 kilometers wide. At lower levels are river forests, at mid-levels are mixed rain forests, and higher up is a mist forest with thick ferns and mosses. Mount Nimba is home to many mammals, including chimpanzees, bongo, forest buffalo, Jentink's duikers, leopards, golden cats, and the very rare pygmy hippopotamus. Pythons are common, and the most famous amphibian in the park is the small viviparous toad. It is a humid climate; December through March is the dry season. Because of contrasting air currents through the area, tornadoes—which are rarely found outside the United States—occur here in March and April.

Students will enjoy studying the animals that live here; you can also have them study the climate and terrain.

Senegal

Djoudj National Bird Sanctuary

Conservateur
Park national des Oiseaux de Djoudj
B P80
Saint Louis

The Senegal River, which flows through the Djoudj Bird Sanctuary, is the first permanent water source that migrating birds from Europe and Asia encounter as they fly from the Sahara Desert. The area is an ancient alluvial bed and is an immense wetland with islands, marshes, rice fields, and prairies. There are grasses, thistles, and river forests that have adapted to the climate. More than two hundred species of native birds and more than one hundred species of migratory birds are found at the Djoudj Bird Sanctuary, including herons, egrets, storks, ibis, pelicans, gulls, terns, ducks, godwits, and flamingos. Djoudj Bird Sanctuary is in a tropical climate zone, with one month of heavy rain, and drought the rest of the year.

Of course Djoudj is a perfect choice for studying birds, but consider also some of the projects involving plant life and water sources.

Niokolo-Koba National Park

Parc Conservateur
PN Niokolo-Koba
Tamba-Counda, BP37

Niokolo-Koba National Park is a conglomeration of three game reserves where two climatic belts meet. It is located on the Gambia River on more than eight hundred thousand hectares of mostly flat land. There is lush and varied vegetation, including savannas with tall grasses, marshes, termite stacks, bamboo, mahogany trees, fig trees, butter trees, palm trees, and gallery forests. Niokolo is home to 350 species of birds: guinea fowl, francolins, bustards, larks, magpies, mannikins, weaver birds, hornbills, herons, storks, and violet turacos. Simenti Pool is a favorite bird-watching area. Mammals include kobs, baboons, hyenas, civets, lions, giraffes, and buffalo. Elephants are rare. The area is uninhabited by people, and with its diverse flora and fauna and abundant birds, Niokolo is a popular site for scientific research.

Participation in plant life and wildlife projects would go well with a study of this park.

United Republic of Tanzania

Kilimanjaro National Park

Chief Park Warden
PO Box 96
Marangu

Near the equator is Kilimanjaro, Africa's highest mountain. Three peaks had formed out of this rift valley in the past, but two collapsed and only Kilimanjaro remains. A burst of volcanic activity has brought the mountain to its present level of 5,895 meters. It rises in a perfect cone shape from the plains, and it is perennially snowcapped and dotted with numerous small glaciers and small morainal lakes. Kilimanjaro is still an active volcano. Life zones change with elevation. The lower slopes are home to the Chagga tribe, which lives on small farmsteads with irrigated water canals. From two thousand to three thousand meters, there is a cloud forest. Above this elevation are open forests of heather and moorland, and an alpine desert begins at four thousand meters. Kilimanjaro is home to many animals, including monkeys, leopards, eland, rhinoceroses, buffalo, and elephants. A five-day guided hike brings travelers up to the summit of Kilimanjaro for spectacular views.

Kilimanjaro is perfect for volcano projects as well as other geology projects, but don't overlook wildlife studies as well as studies of changes in plant life that occur in different elevations.

Ngorongoro Conservation Area

Ngorongoro Conservation Area Authority
PO Box 2
Ngorongoro Crater Arusha

Ngorongoro is one of the world's greatest geological wonders. This twenty-kilometer-wide volcanic crater with its six-hundred-meter-high walls contains lush vegetation and nearly every species of wildlife in East Africa. Ngorongoro's volcanic activity dates back two and a half million years to when the volcanic cone eventually collapsed into the caldera, which is still visible today. Further volcanic eruptions created the small hills called hillocks throughout the park. Ngoronogoro became a preserved area in 1951. It is connected to the Serengeti Plain, and many animals migrate between the two preserves. Amongst the wildlife seen in Ngorongoro are flamingos, lions, Thomson's gazelles, reedbucks, zebras, rhinoceroses, buffalo, wildebeests, and elephants. The local Maasai tribe uses the land for grazing cattle.

Ngorongoro is another perfect site for the study of volcanic activity as well as its effects on the surrounding terrain.

Selous Game Reserve

The Wildlife Division
Ministry of Natural Resources and Tourism
PO Box 1994
Dar-es-Salaam

Covering 54,600 square kilometers, Selous Game Reserve is the world's largest reserve, most of which remains unexplored. It was originally established in 1922 as a hunting reserve. Flowing through Selous is the the huge Rufiji River, which is east of Africa's largest catchment area. At the north end of the reserve, where the Rufiji River meets the Ruaha River, is the park's best-known feature, Stiegler's Gorge. The gorge is one hundred meters deep and wide, and there's a cable car that crosses it. Most of the park's lodges are located near Stiegler's Gorge. Selous contains the world's largest concentration of wild dogs, crocodiles, hippopotamuses, buffalo, and elephants. There are also antelope, lions, and rhinoceroses in the park, as well as more than one thousand species of birds.

Students can study Stiegler's Gorge from a geological perspective or research the many different animal species that live in this preserve.

Serengeti National Park

The Wildlife Division
Ministry of Natural Resources and Tourism
PO Box 1994
Dar-es-Salaam

Located just north of the equator, this vast wilderness of semiarid grasslands and woodlands boasts the greatest natural wildlife spectacle on Earth. Within Sergengeti are up to 14,763 square kilometers of savanna plains, woodlands near rivers, and montane forests. There are also granite rock conglomerations called kopjes, isolated mountains, and craters from extinct volcanoes. In the world-renowned Olduvai Gorge are the oldest known fossil remains of prehistoric man and vertebrate animals. The park's wildlife demonstrates a perfect predator-to-prey relationship, and completing the full ecosystem of Serengeti are the adjacent Masai Mara, Ngorongoro, and Lake Victoria conservation areas.

Millions of hoofed animals roam the endless savanna plains, following a clockwise migration route. Wildebeests, gazelles, and zebras are the most numerous animals. Masai cattle herders are allowed to graze their animals in the park. Other animals commonly seen in the park are crocodiles, topi, jackals, hyenas, cheetahs, leopards, eland, antelope, rhinoceroses, hippopotamuses, giraffes, and Africa's densest population of lions. Poaching, especially for rhinoceroses and their horns, continues to be a problem in the park. Birds include ostriches, bustards, vultures, and flamingos. Serengeti has a subtropical climate that varies with elevation.

Students can participate in projects involving geology, geography, plant life, and wildlife in their study of this diverse park.

Democratic Republic of the Congo (Zaire)

Garamba National Park

Conservateur Principal
Parc National de la Garamba
Nagero, BP 141
Isiro

Garamba National Park was originally set up in 1938 to protect the northern white rhinoceros, one of the most threatened species in the world. In 1963, there were 1,300 white rhinoceroses in the park, but because of wars and poaching, by 1984 the population had fallen to just 15. Since then, because of antipoaching efforts, the population has increased to thirty-one. Other mammals in the park include baboons, leopards, lions, antelope, giraffes, buffalo, and elephants. Garamba National Park is situated on an ancient peneplain, with vast undulating plateaus and isolated hills. There are woodlands, wooded savannas, fire-swept grasslands, and gallery forests along the Garamba River. The climate is semimoist and tropical during the rainy season, and it is dry from November to March.

Have your students research the current status of the white rhinoceros in Garamba National Park.

Virunga National Park and Kahuzi-Biega National Park

Virunga
Parc National des Virunga
Station de la Rwindi
Rwindi, D/S Goma, Kivu,
Institut Zairois pour la Conservation de la Nature (IZCH)
BP 868
Kinshasa 1

Virunga and Kahuzi-Biega are two parks located in Central Africa. They contain one of the last strongholds of the mountain gorilla and the eastern lowland gorilla.

Virunga, at an elevation up to 5,109 meters, is an extremely active geological region, with deltas, plateaus, plains, glaciers, snowfields, and active volcanoes. The park claims to have the widest variety of habitats in Africa. It contains unusual vegetation, including bamboo and giant lobelia. In the 1960s, up to fifteen thousand mountain gorillas may have lived here; now, because of poaching, only about three hundred are left. Other animals include elephants and about twenty-five thousand hippopotamuses. A tremendous amount of rain falls in Virunga.

In Kahuzi lives the famous eastern lowland gorilla, which is the type of gorilla that appeared in the movie *Gorillas in the Mist*. There are more than two hundred fifty in the park within twenty-five different families. The park provides tours to see the gorillas, but since many gorillas have died because of exposure to human diseases, the park has had to limit the size of its tour groups. Kahuzi is mostly thick, lowland jungles.

Have students research further the status of gorillas in these two parks, including ways in which human activity has helped and hindered their populations.

Australia and New Zealand

Australia

Great Barrier Reef

Great Barrier Reef Marine Park Authority
PO Box 1379
Townsville, QLD 4810
Phone: 61-77-500-700

More than two thousand kilometers long, the Great Barrier Reef is the world's greatest conglomeration of coral reefs and shoals. The area includes many cays, reefs, and islands. Around the islands are archaeological sites, shipwrecks, and lighthouses. The sea is always warm, and the water provides a fantastic, unobstructed habitat for unique marine life, with more than 1,500 species of fish, 300 species of hard reef-biting coral, 400 species of mollusks, and 400 species of sponges, anemones, worms, crustaceans, and echinoderms. The area is also a feeding and nesting ground for endangered dugongs, green and loggerhead turtles, humpback whales, reef sharks, and great white sharks. An incredible variety of birds—cormorants, gulls, waders, ospreys, pelicans, herons, and sea eagles—live in the Great Barrier Reef. There are grasslands, shrubs, and forests on various islands in the park. Because of the wide varieties of plants and animals that inhabit the area, much scientific research takes place here. Snorkeling and scuba diving are very popular activities in this park.

Your students will enjoy projects involving geography as well as the park's wildlife, most notably the great white shark.

Kakadu National Park

Department of the Environment, Sports, and Territories
GPO Box 787
Canberra, ACT 2601
Phone: 06-274-1111

Since the movie *Crocodile Dundee* was filmed in Kakadu National Park in the 1980s, the park has become well-known. It is one of the premier national parks of the world, and it has had the rare honor of being qualified for World Heritage for both cultural and natural values. Kakadu has one of the world's best collections of rock art, with more than one thousand recorded painting sites. Aboriginal peoples still live indigenously in the park. Rock escarpments, major rivers, and large waterfalls are found in Kakadu, and there are wetlands, grasslands, mangrove forests, and monsoonal rain forests. Inhabiting the park are more than 280 species of birds, including waders, rare parrots, and the white-throated grass wren, and there are frogs, fish, and numerous insects. There are also many fresh- and saltwater crocodiles, as well as a variety of other reptiles. Throughout most of the year, the park is hot and humid, and there are seasonal monsoonal rains. Kakadu has extensive tourist facilities.

Your students will have fun with projects involving plant life and wildlife, as well as the ancient painting sites.

Uluru-Kata Tjuta National Park

The Chairman
Uluru-Kata Tjuta Board of Management
PO Box 3566
Alice Springs, NT 0871

Uluru contains the world-famous Ayer's Rock and the nearby Olga rocks, which rise high above the red standstone plain of the area. Ayer's Rock is a huge sandstone monolith, reaching 340 meters in height and nine kilometers in circumference, and it is surrounded by springs, caves, and aboriginal artwork. The Olgas are thirty-six domelike rocks that are up to five hundred meters high. Ayer's Rock and the Olgas have weathered over time, and they appear to change colors as the sun sets. The rocks extend well below the earth's surface. More than four hundred species of plants are found in Uluru, including eucaplypti, spinifexes, and desert oaks, as well as many types of wildflowers, grasses, and shrubs. Mammals include bats, echidnas, dingoes, wallabies, kangaroos, and several introduced species. Amongst the many reptiles are geckos, goannas, dragons, perentie lizards, thorny devils, pythons, and eight species of poisonous snakes. Uluru is home to 150 species of birds, such as pink cockatoos, magpies, mulga parrots, kestrels, and falcons. The local aboriginal tribe, Agana, which has lived in Uluru for more than ten thousand years, manages the park. The area is generally hot and dry, with brief heavy rains.

Uluru offers excellent opportunities for geology projects, along with activities exploring the plant life and wildlife.

Tasmanian Wilderness

Tasmanian Parks and Wildlife Service
GPO Box 44A
Hobart TAS 7001

The Tasmanian Wilderness is the last great remaining temperate forest wilderness of the world. The park system consists of a group of national parks: Cradle Mountain, Lake St. Clair, Franklin-Gordon Rivers, Southwest, and the Walls of Jerusalem. Within the park system are rugged peaks, numerous lakes, buttongrass plains, moorlands, alpine heathland, rain forests, eucalypt forests, wild rivers, canyons, caves, gorges, evidence of glaciation, and rock art up to thirty thousand years old. There are many rare and endangered species of plant and animal life. The Tasmania area broke off from the supercontinent— Gondwanaland—many millions of years ago. The separation created many endemic plant species. There are Huon pines up to two thousand years old, as well as many mosses, ferns, and cushion plants. Tasmania is the last refuge for many animals that once lived all over Australia. All of the world's remaining large predatory marsupials live in the park system, including Tasmanian devils, eastern quolls, spotted-tail quolls, and, possibly, the Tasmanian tiger. There are also wallabies, opossums, pademelons, and wombats. In Western Tasmania, the weather is unpredictable, and snow, hail, sleet, and fog occur all year long. There has been little human intrusion in the park.

Students will enjoy learning about the exotic wildlife of the Tasmanian Wilderness, as well as the ancient ties to Gondwanaland.

New Zealand

Te Wahipounamu–Southwest New Zealand

Director, Planning and External Agencies Division
Department of Conservation
PO Box 10-240
Wellington, New Zealand
Phone: 04-471-0766

In the southwestern region of South Island in New Zealand, this massive, temperate wilderness encompasses four national parks: Fjordland, Westland, Mount Aspiring, and Mount Cook. The remote area of Fjordland alone is one of the world's largest national parks. Features of the parks include glowworm caves, hot springs, fjords, large névés (areas where snow and ice are converted into glaciers), glacial rivers, waterfalls, ocean moraines, remote wild beaches, temperate rain forests, and massive glaciers. Southwest New Zealand has experienced repeated glaciation, and evidence of such glaciation appears in rock formations and successive plant growth. The glaciers extend to nearly twenty-seven kilometers long and some run into sea-level rain forests. Extremely heavy rain falls each year on the west sides of the mountains, and there is abundant snowfall at higher elevations.

Plants exist in vertical botanical zones. There are wildflowers, ferns, shrubs, and pines. Sea animals include penguins, seals, and dolphins. Because of the wide range of bird habitats in Southwest New Zealand, there are many birds, including keas, kakapos, kiwis, takahes, kakas, grebes, and herons. The area remains as the only habitat for the takahe, which is a bird the world once considered extinct.

An overabundance of tourism, noise pollution from scenic flights, nonnative opossums and other animals that were introduced by man, road developments, and water exportations all threaten the diversity of the four parks of Southwest New Zealand.

This is a perfect area for students to explore the effects of human activity on an environment.

Tongariro National Park

Director, Planning and External Agencies Division
Department of Conservation
PO Box 10-420
Wellington, New Zealand
Phone: 04-471-0726

Tongariro is a spectacular alpine park on New Zealand's northern island on the rim of the Pacific Basin. The area has a long volcanic history, and the park has three active volcanoes: Mount Ruapehu (2,792 meters), Ngauruho (2,291 meters), and Tongariro (1,968 meters). Mount Ruapehu has had many recorded eruptions in the past 125 years. It is one of the few volcanoes in the world with a hot crater lake surrounded by active glaciers. Tongariro park has a fifteen-kilometer-long lava flow, a mud flow plain, hot springs, lakes, numerous waterfalls, deep gorges, grasslands, desertlike lava plains, and dense forests. The park has snow all winter, and throughout the year it remains wet and experiences extreme temperature changes. There are 470 plant species in the park: at lower elevations are rimu, miro, and beech forests; at middle elevations are mountain totara and mountain beech; and at higher elevations are red tussocks. At the highest elevations are meadows and bogs. Birds are found mostly on the lower slopes and include kiwis, tuis, kakas, warblers, pigeons, and fantails. Only exotic animals exist in Tongariro, and they include rabbits, pigs, opossums, and red deer.

Here is another perfect site for the study of volcanic activity, particularly because it has a hot crater lake surrounded by active glaciers. Your students can also participate in projects involving the glaciers.

Appendix B: The National Park Fair

· ·

Each year, my students and I put on a national park fair. It's a huge undertaking, but well worth the effort. Depending upon your needs, you can hold the fair as part of the science curriculum or social studies curriculum, or it can be integrated into several different subjects. Your fair can be held indoors or outdoors, depending on the climate where you live. It can take place during school hours, in the evening, or on the weekend. Whatever you decide, the most important thing is to plan ahead as many weeks or months as you can. This appendix will give you some guidelines and suggestions for conducting your fair, but don't forget to use your own imagination and intuition—as well as your students'—to make your fair unique and successful.

Park Introduction Statements

Several weeks before the national park fair, I have my ranger groups write up Park Introduction Statements. These statements serve as visitor introductions to the parks, and they also help the student rangers focus on their goals for the fair and their purposes for being rangers for their parks.

Each ranger group is required to create Park Introduction Statements that contain the following information:

- a brief description of the park
- who is in the park ranger group and what the group is doing
- ranger goals for the park
- what rangers need to tell visitors about helping or saving the park

Park Introduction Statement

We the rangers at Galapagos National Park are here to give you as much information as we can about our unique, isolated park. Our ranger group consists of Hanna Millard, Alisha Crandall, and Casey Abels. We feel very lucky to represent Galapagos. It is such an incredibly beautiful place, and the wildlife—including iguanas and giant tortoises—is amazing. We've done everything we can to get to know our park well and to provide you with descriptions and demonstrations that you'll remember. If you ever get to visit Galapagos, you'll know what a special place it is. We hope it stays that way and that tourists don't leave any trash on the island. Hopefully, one day you'll join us on one of the thirteen Galapagos Islands!

FIGURE B–1: PARK INTRODUCTION STATEMENT

I take these Park Introduction Statements through the normal writing process of outlining, writing, peer editing, and developing into a final draft. In the end, a typed and enlarged statement can be posted right above the main window at the ranger station. Figure B–1 is a sample park introduction statement.

Ranger Stations

At least two weeks before the national park fair, I get my students started on planning the "ranger stations" that they will create for their park demonstrations during the fair.

My students and I start by making a draft plan on the chalkboard of a sample ranger station. We look at the projects we have done as shown on the Project List and Evaluation Form, then estimate the dimensions the ranger station should be to best accommodate the projects. I note on the draft plan where the various projects should be placed in and around the ranger station. We include a window or area where rangers can talk to the visitors who come by the station. Space is also provided around the station for displaying posters, creating "nature trails," doing readings, and so on. Once I have completed the final draft plan on the chalkboard, I have a student copy the plan onto a sheet of paper. I make photocopies of this student drawing and distribute them to the student ranger groups. The students can take the drawings home and work with them when building their own ranger stations.

The students' ranger stations should be designed so they somehow relate to their parks. I encourage my students to be creative and come up with their own unique designs. The ranger stations students have made and brought to school are so creative I always look forward to seeing them and love taking pictures of them. Some of the stations my rangers have done in the past include the following:

- an A-frame cabin built out of wood shingles
- tent caves complete with tunnels and cave formations
- junglelike stations cut from cardboard boxes with jungle scenes painted on
- mountain-shaped stations cut from cardboard and painted to look like erupting volcanoes

Many of these stations are built at home with help, and I encourage that. I like the idea of parents and children working together for the students' school projects. Most likely, parents will be doing at least some of the work and helping to acquire supplies. For those students who might get less help at home, I bring in a stack of refrigerator boxes that they can use to construct their ranger stations at school.

Because of the lack of space at my school, I have my students wait to bring their ranger stations to school until just two to three days before the national park fair. Stations should be dropped off by parents and stored in a section of a multipurpose room.

When it is time to set up and display the ranger stations, I gather my class in a circle in our multipurpose room. I hold a hat that contains slips of paper with the park names written on them. I pull a park name from the hat and ask that group to tell us about their station and if they have any special needs we should consider when setting up their displays. For example, some groups might need a corner of the room to support their stations, while others might need extra chairs and tables. Once that group describes its station and its needs, I let the members go set up their station. While I continue to pull park names from the hat, parents help move and set up the stations.

Once the stations are set up, my students and I gather again to discuss appropriate places for all their displays within the stations. We decide where park names would best fit on the stations. I allow my students more flexibility in deciding where to display their other projects in and around their stations. I have my students draw quick sketches showing where all their projects will be displayed. Once I approve of their sketches, I let them set up the displays and put on any finishing touches to their projects.

I found in the past that ranger groups sometimes made unhealthy comparisons between their ranger station creations by judging whose was best and why. Therefore, I no longer evaluate the stations in the final grades on the national park fair. I always stress to my students that it's the *projects*, not the actual stations, that will be judged.

Other Fair Projects

Costumes and Uniforms

About one week before the fair, I brainstorm with my students some ideas for costumes or uniforms that they can wear during the national park fair. Students can wear clothes based on the country in which their park is located. They can make costumes that relate to the geography or other features of their parks; for example, students studying mountainous Sagarmatha National Park in Nepal can dress like mountaineers. They can also make their own ranger T-shirts and badges. Another idea is to have the students order from their parks T-shirts with the park names and perhaps pictures and logos printed on them. You can imagine how excited rangers are to wear a shirt that says "Kakadu National Park" on it along with a picture of a crocodile.

Sensory Nature Trails

A few years ago I was in Anza Borrego Desert State Park in California and a ranger friend of mine was leading a blindfolded group of youngsters on a sensory nature walk amidst dozens of very thorny cacti. I tied a scarf around my eyes and joined them, and I quickly realized how much more I could learn about an area without my eyesight. From this experience, I came up with the following idea for my students.

I start by having the student rangers select ten interesting objects that relate to their park. I tell them the objects should be ones that could be experienced through the senses. The following are some examples of objects that could be used.

- ice (to represent glaciers)
- pinecones
- edible foods (make sure the foods students want to bring in are safe to eat)
- antlers
- creek sounds (recorded)
- leaves and needles
- crab shells
- feathers
- wind (from a fan)

- rocks
- water

Then the students develop a poster of the objects. First they draw a picture of each object that they have selected. Underneath the picture of each object, I have them write where the object is found in their park and/or how it relates to the park. Once a draft of the poster is completed, they get permission from me to create a final poster.

The students use the information from their posters to set up a little sensory "nature trail" on which to take visitors during the national park fair. The trail can be up to twenty feet long, depending upon available space, and each object should be set somewhere along the trail. I've had some students lay string to denote the path of the trail, and they've connected the objects to the string. Trails can also be marked in the multipurpose room using rows of chairs or with masking tape directly on the floor. Trails can also be made outdoors. At the end of the trail, the student rangers display the poster of the objects.

During the fair, student rangers ask visitors if they want to take a little walk through the park. First, a visitor is blindfolded, then a student ranger guides him or her down the trail, where the visitor gets to touch, smell, taste, and/or listen to each object. The visitor tries to guess what each object is. At the end of the trail, the visitor removes the blindfold, and the student ranger can share the poster with the visitor by pointing out the objects and explaining how they relate to the park.

These sensory nature trails are always one of the most popular parts of the students' ranger stations, and young visitors especially like this activity.

Language Posters

In many cases, the students are learning about a park that is in a foreign country, and usually people of those foreign countries speak a language other than English. I have my students who have parks in non-English-speaking countries learn some of the words of the prominent language.

I have my students list ten to twenty of the most common natural objects found in their parks, such as the following:

- waterfall
- river
- fossil
- tree
- fish
- cave
- rhinoceros

- glacier
- mountain
- rain forest

Next, I have them look up the words in a language dictionary or traveler's phrase book. Then I have them create posters titled "How to Say It in _____." Down the left side of the poster, the students write the names of the objects in English, and down the right side they write the words in the native language of the country.

Visitor Speeches

Before the fair, I have my student ranger groups make brief visitor speeches about the national park fair to other classrooms. The purpose of these speeches is to let other classes know about the fair, and the speeches also help my students practice speaking to others about their parks in preparation for the fair.

I ask my students to do the following during these speeches:

- introduce themselves
- talk about the date, time, and purpose of the national park fair
- briefly describe their park
- show one poster or other project that their group has done for the fair
- ask the audience if there are any questions
- encourage the class to come to the fair

I also encourage my students to wear their ranger costumes or uniforms when they give their speeches.

Before delivering their speeches, I have my students practice the elements of good public speaking. We work on eye contact, speaking volume, voice projection, use of feeling, and appropriate pauses in speaking. We also talk about how to answer questions from the audience. I have my students practice making their speeches in pairs or in small groups, usually standing back from their partner at a distance of about ten feet so they can work on eye contact and voice projection.

Special Presentations for the Fair

Special presentations are activities that students perform for an audience during the national park fair for only a select amount of time. Special presentations include projects, activities, and demonstrations that can only be done a few times because of a lack of supplies. Erosion Trays, Wind Erosion, and Park Creation Legends, as well as reading stories, are examples of special presentations.

Together, my students and I write up a list of all the special presentations that the students will be doing. Then I set up a master presentation schedule so that the presentations are done approximately every ten minutes throughout the fair. On this schedule, we also note where each presentation will be done. Smaller activities or experiments done by one or two students can be done in front of the ranger stations. Larger presentations can be performed on a stage or another area of the multipurpose room, where seating is set up for about twenty people.

To promote their special presentations, I let my students create up to three colorful Special Presentations Poster to display around the multipurpose room as advertisements. A poster shows the name of the park, describes the presentation, and lists the time or times of the presentation.

Just before the fair, I post the master presentation schedule at the staging area and also at the greeters' table. The students can display their poster ads near the greeters' table, at the ranger stations, and in some other appropriate place.

During the fair, I let my students take turns announcing on the school's P. A. system their special presentations about five minutes before they are scheduled to begin. Students also tell the visitors at their stations about their upcoming performances. When students need to leave their ranger stations to do special demonstrations, they shut down their stations posting a sign that states "Closed for ten minutes."

Getting Ready for the Visitors

If you have had a large park map set up in your classroom, put it up in the multipurpose room where visitors to the national park fair can see it. You can also include a banner that says "Welcome to the World's Best Places!"

Set up a greeters' table at the entrance to the fair to welcome visitors. Two to three students at a time can sit at this table on a rotating basis. At the table, provide visitors with the following items:

- a list of the parks
- Visitor Information Pamphlets created by the students
- a Special Presentations Poster created by the students

During the fair, I often let parents, teachers, and other adult visitors walk around and evaluate projects using the Project Rubric forms. So, at the greeters' table, I provide a stack of the forms, along with a list of projects that can be evaluated.

After the greeters' table is set up, I gather my students around the greeters' table and we talk about what their responsibilities are when they greet guests. I remind them to be enthusiastic, helpful, and prepared to answer any questions visitors might have.

When everything is nearly set up for the fair, I gather my student rangers together for a class tour of the fair so they can see what it will look like to visitors. We walk around to the different ranger stations and I have each group briefly tell us about its own station. I carry a project checklist with me and ask to see where various projects are. I also ask my students to give their classmates any last-minute constructive feedback they might have for each ranger station.

Videotaping and Photographing the Fair

I always have a parent volunteer videotape the national park fair. I give the volunteer a list of the items I want him or her to videotape. The items on this list include the following:

- the greeters' table
- special posters, ads, murals, etc.
- each ranger station
- a brief interview of each ranger at his or her own station, with a parent acting as the interviewer
- dramatic presentations
- experiments and activities
- some of the visitors to the fair, as well as visitor comments

Often the person videotaping spends an hour or more gathering all of this information on tape. My goal each year has been to edit the tape down to about a half-hour show of the fair.

I also take dozens of photographs of the students doing the projects and activities before and during the fair. I especially like taking photos of the student ranger groups in front of their own ranger stations.

After the fair, my students and I enjoy watching the videotape and looking at the photos. I also save the videotapes and photos from past years and share them with my current students when I first introduce them to the World's Best Places.

Taking Home Projects and Stations After the Fair

Once the fair is over, there is still work to do. Stations must be dismantled and evaluations completed. I even recommend some follow-up activities.

First, I have my students decide what to do with their ranger stations and group projects. I usually suggest to the ranger groups that the student who did the most work on a particular ranger station or project should be the one who gets to take it home. If students need help deciding, I will figure out a fair way to make the decision. I have the students arrange with their parents to take the ranger stations home as soon as possible.

Follow-Up Activities

It's a good idea to reinforce learning—and minimize letdown!—with a few follow-up activities after the fair.

Letter Writing

I like to follow up the park fair with a letter-writing assignment. I have each student write letters to his or her park, thanking park employees for sending the information and also describing what the student did for his or her study of the park. They can include pictures of themselves in front of their ranger stations at the fair.

Student Evaluation

I like to take time after the park fair to have my students evaluate their projects and the fair. This is a good time to view the video, if you made one, and any photographs you took. For the evaluation, I have my students first write their answers to these questions:

- What are you most proud of?
- What would you do differently?
- What park display did you like the most and why?
- What are your suggestions for improving the study of the World's Best Places?
- Do you have any suggestions for me, the teacher?

After the students answer the questions, we discuss them as a class.

Vacation Diaries

For this project, the students plan their own pretend vacations during which they travel to several of the parks. I have my students gather into groups of about three people, and I give each group a copy of a world map. The students then mark on their maps up to five of the World's Best Places that the class studied that they would like to visit.

The students in each group then work together to plan one big vacation during which they would visit all their chosen parks. They mark on their maps one continuous path showing the routes they would take to get to each park. They also add arrows to the loop that indicate the direction in which they would travel. Then the students create vacation diaries in which they describe day-to-day accounts of their imaginary trips. Information in the diaries can include the following:

- what the travelers would need to take with them
- modes of transportation they would use (these must be realistic)
- where they would stay
- what they would eat
- what they would see and do at each park
- what realistic adventures they would be involved in during a visit to the park—perhaps an encounter with a grizzly bear on a hiking trail, going white-water rafting down a wild river, or spending a night lost on a freezing-cold glacier (I do discourage violent stories such as being eaten by a crocodile or being killed by lava flow!)

The students share their vacation diaries with the class by reading their daily entries. They also show the class their planned travel routes on a large world map.

Vacation Game Boards

For this activity, the ranger groups create game boards that are based on taking vacations at their parks. The boards will be similar to the Endangered Species Game Boards described in Chapter 3. The game board should include a lightly drawn background picture, which can be a copy of the single park feature that best symbolizes the park. This symbol could be a geographical feature, an animal, or a plant. On top of the background picture, students can create a course of twenty-five to fifty one-inch squares or two-inch squares that snake across the game board.

When my students first create their game boards, I have them start by sketching a rough draft of the game board background and course on an 8½ x 11" sheet of paper. Once I approve the rough draft, I have my students create their game boards on a poster board that is approximately 2 x 3'. My students first use pencil to sketch in the background picture and course on the board. They also use pencil to write information in each square as explained later.

On about one-half of the squares, which are chosen at random along the game board course, have your students create "move forward" and "take another turn" steps that a player would follow when landing on the selected squares. These squares should contain *positive* experiences a traveler would have when vacationing in the park. Some examples could be:

- You got the last room at the hotel—move forward one space

- You saw wild elephants in the distance—take another turn
- You met up with a local expert tour guide—move forward two spaces
- You found that the money exchange rate was favorable—move forward five spaces

On about one-fourth of the squares, the students can create "move backward" or "skip a turn" squares that contain *negative* travel experiences. These squares are also chosen at random along the course. Some examples could be:

- You got a flat tire while on the jungle tour—lose a turn
- Your hut was infested with mosquitoes—move back one space
- You got sick from drinking unfiltered water—lose two turns
- Your flight was delayed for two hours because of torrential rains—move back two spaces

On all the remaining squares, the students can write in *neutral* travel information such as "One million visitors a year come to this park" or "It takes 3 hours to drive from one end of the park to the other." When players land on any of these spaces, they simply read the information.

After my students create their entire game boards using pencil, I have them play a practice round of the game to see if they are able to finish it in a reasonable amount of time and to see if the information written in the squares is easy to understand. They finalize their game boards by tracing over their pencil lines, drawings, and words with black marking pens, and they color in the background drawing with colored marking pens. We always laminate the finished game boards.

I have my students make the game pieces and draw pictures on them that relate to vacationing in the park. For example, a set of game pieces might have pictures of hiking boots, binoculars, suitcases, and cameras. The students can either use store-bought dice or they can make their own dice by cutting patterns from poster board that can be folded into cubes.

I have my students set up their games in different sections of the class, and students take turns playing the games. I have one student ranger from each park stay by his or her own game board to supervise play and answer any questions.

In Conclusion

Here are a few last thoughts I like to leave with my students. Perhaps these thoughts can also be shared with your students.

The World's Best Places need our help. Help begins with knowledge, and I hope knowledge will keep us connected to the parks. There are international organizations and journals that can keep students informed of the goings-on at their parks. I share a list of some of these groups with my students (see Appendix C). Many of these organizations offer ways to stay involved and in touch by joining clubs, reading journals, and sponsoring adoptions. I further promote this idea with a field trip to a bookstore or library, where we look for books on endangered species, world parks, and travel.

Somewhere in the students' packets of information, there may be suggestions for further reading. There may also be information on books, T-shirts, and souvenirs that can be purchased directly from the parks. I point this information out to my students.

Between these books and the information my students have found in their park brochures, I compose a list of resources to which students can write for more information and to find out what's happening in their parks. I type up a list of the resources and hand out copies to my students at the end of the year.

I've had students come back to visit me the next fall proudly showing me what they have ordered from their park's catalog. I've also had students come back years later to tell me that they are looking forward to visiting the park for which they had been a student ranger soon—or that they just did! Nothing makes me happier.

Will the planet make it? Will our World's Best Places last? Will the plants, animals, and magnificent features of each park survive? As long as there is a spark in the eyes of our students, and we continue to teach them about their world, there is hope. As Edward Abbey, a famous environmental author and former park ranger, once said, "The idea of wilderness needs no defense, only more defenders."

There is nothing more wonderful than seeing my students become knowledgeable about the World's Best Places and so protective of them. My students have been transformed into park stewards, and I hope they will enthusiastically carry that torch into the future. Thank you for seeing this project through, contributing to a global vision, and giving the World's Best Places a fighting chance.

Appendix C: Related Organizations

. . . .

Earthwatch Institute
3 Clock Tower Place, Suite 100
Box 75
Maynard, MA 01754
(978) 461-0081
Website: *www.earthwatch.org*
E-mail: *info@earthwatch.org*

Environmental Defense Fund
257 Park Avenue
New York, NY 10010
(212) 505-2375
Website: *www.edf.org*
E-mail: *contact@environmentaldefense.org*

Friends of the Earth
1025 Vermont Avenue N.W., Suite 300
Washington, D.C. 20005
(202) 783-7400
Website: *www.foe.org*
E-mail: *foe@foe.org*

Greenpeace
1436 U Street N.W.
Washington, D.C. 20009

(202) 462-1177

Website: *www.greenpeace.org*

E-mail: *none available*

National Parks Conservation Association

1300 Nineteenth Street, N.W.

Suite 300

Washington, D.C. 20036

(202) 223-6722

Website: *www.npca.org*

E-mail: *npca@npca.org*

National Research Council

2101 Consitution Avenue, N.W.

Washington, D.C. 20418

(202) 334-2000

Website: *www.nas.edu*

E-mail: *none available*

Rainforest Action Network

221 Pine Street, Suite 500

San Francisco, CA 94104

(800) 398-4404

Website: *www.ran.org*

E-mail: *rainforest@ran.org*

Sierra Club

85 2nd Street, 2nd Floor

San Francisco, CA 94105-3441

(415) 977-5500

Website: *www.sierraclub.org*

E-mail: *webmaster@sierraclub.org*

UNESCO Association of the U.S.A.

5815 Lawton Ave.

Oakland, CA 94618-1510

(510) 654-4638

Website: *www.unesco.org*

E-mail: *uausa@pacbell.net*

UNESCO World Heritage Secretariat
Division of Ecological Sciences
UNESCO
7, Place de Fontenoy
75352 Paris 07 SP France
International Phone: 33 1 45 68 10 00
Website: *none available*
E-mail: *none available*

Wilderness Society
900 17th Street, N.W.
Washington, D.C. 20006-2596
(800) 843-9453
Website: *www.wilderness.org*
E-mail: *none available*

World Wildlife Fund
1250 24th Street, N.W.
P.O. Box 97180
Washington, D.C. 20077-7180
(202) 293-4800
Website: *www.worldwildlife.org*
E-mail: *none available*

Appendix D: Forms to Photocopy

Following are blank copies of the Project List and Evaluation Form and the Project Rubric that teachers can photocopy for their own use.

THE WORLD'S BEST PLACES
Project List and Evaluation Form

Ranger: Park:

Projects and Activities	Draft Completed	Final Completed	Grade	Notes
Introduction Projects				
Wildlife Projects				
Plant Life Projects				

Geography and Geology Projects				
National Park Fair Projects				
After-the-Fair Projects				
FINAL GRADE *(0 = Redo/No Credit)*				

PROJECT RUBRIC

Student: Project:

Date: Evaluator:

DESCRIPTION	SCORE 6 is highest and 1 is lowest; 0 is no credit
Attractive	
Neat	
Colorful	
Realistic illustrations	
Accurate spelling	
Relevant information	
Other	
Total Score	
Average Score	
Grade*	

*GRADE: 6 = A 5 = B 4 = B 3 = C 2 = D 1 = F 0 = Redo/No Credit

COMMENTS